V.S. NAIPAUL

FICTION AND TRAVEL WRITING

Edited by

Rajeshwar Mittapalli
Michael Hensen

ATLANTIC

PUBLISHERS & DISTRIBUTORS (P) LTD

Published by

ATLANTIC

PUBLISHERS & DISTRIBUTORS (P) LTD

B-2, Vishal Enclave, Opp. Rajouri Garden,
New Delhi-110027
Phones : +91-11-25413460, 25429987, 25466842

Sales Office
7/22, Ansari Road, Darya Ganj,
New Delhi-110002
Phones : +91-11-23273880, 23275880, 23280451
Fax : +91-11-23285873
Web : www.atlanticbooks.com
E-mail : info@atlanticbooks.com

Branch Office
5, Nallathambi Street, Wallajah Road,
Chennai-600002
Phones : +91-44-64611085, 32413319
E-mail : chennai@atlanticbooks.com

ISBN 978-81-269-0172-2

Printed in India
at Nice Printing Press, Delhi

PREFACE

The Nobel award to Naipaul has given us a fresh occasion to reassess his contribution to fiction and travel literature. Among the reasons for awarding him the Prize the Nobel Committee noted his insistence on writing about "peripheral people" with "suppressed histories," his dealing extensively with shifting identities, roots, homes and the changing realities of migrants. The Swedish Academy praised his distinct style in which "the customary distinctions between fiction and non-fiction are of subordinate importance." These thematic and generic aspects of Naipaul's works reveal a cosmos of borderlines, and need to be gone into.

The subject-matter of Naipaul's novels and travel writings is the constant negotiation of where the individual is situated: country or city, inside the community or outside, within tradition or outside, and in the colonised world or post-colonial societies. What emerges out of these writings is Naipaul's stance on displaced individuals, uprooted and without a distinct place called 'home' but longing for it all the same. In 1981, Bharati Mukherjee claimed, "his writing is about unhousing and remaining unhoused" and this holds good for both his early and later works. Even if Mr. Biswas calls the house his own at the end of *A House for Mr. Biswas*, he remains vulnerable *vis-à-vis* his economic situation, and his "unhoused" condition is brought home by the fact that he will always be at the mercy of social and political forces and his own personal compulsions. This is true of many of Naipaul's later fictional figures who remain unhoused in themselves and are, therefore, located on the borderlines of fixed and shifting identities, living 'half-lives' prescribed by the colonial and post-colonial experience.

In formal terms, Naipaul experiments along the boundaries of fiction and non-fiction, in particular travel writing and autobiography. His novels, as many critics have pointed out, are characterised by his own experiences, and deeply influenced by his father's writings and the ethos of the community he belongs to. In his travel writings, he frequently tries to keep himself out of the picture, but still constitutes the soul of the narrative and its organisation.

The blurring of the boundaries is a significant factor in the evaluation of Naipaul by critics and discerning readers. While some claim that he is among the "finest living novelists writing in English," one who has a "uniquely authoritative position as an interpreter of colonial societies," others dismiss his works as overshadowed by his political ideology. These latter critics speak of his "ironic eclecticism and brahmanical aloofness." Naipaul's status as a writer was and is frequently seen as polemical and controversial, more so in the aftermath of the Nobel award. Despite a certain penchant on the part of Naipaul for controversy, or perhaps because of it, his works continue to enjoy popularity, and for good reasons. He has created many memorable characters (Man-Man, Mr. Biswas and Ganesh, to name but a few). His prose is highly readable, and his style is distinct to the point of being inimitable.

The articles included in this anthology take up these different thematic strands and elaborate on them. John Thieme looks at the recent history of the Nobel Prize and considers the reasons for Naipaul's winning it. He puts Naipaul's works into perspective by viewing them in relation to those of other Anglophone Caribbean writers such as Walcott and Harris.

Starting from a post-modern and post-colonial standpoint, Stuti Khanna studies some of Naipaul's works as novels of migration and profitably compares them with the novels of Mistry, Rushdie and Selvadurai. She points to the remarkably varied approaches of these authors towards the recurring topics of 'self' and the 'other,' identity and hybridity. In his reading of *A Bend in the River,* Fausto Ciompi relates these concepts to Naipaul's narrative style. He examines point of view and sentence structures as well as the overall rhetorics of the novel, all of which, according to him, indicate the fluidity inherent in the title and in Naipaul's approach towards identity, politics and history. Florence D'Souza inquires into the interface between Naipaul and two of his works (*The Enigma of Arrival* and *Half a Life*), and examines some of the important intertexts used to characterise the protagonist, as well as some of the leitmotifs Naipaul draws upon (such as garden, decay and cobras). Harald Leusmann's article shows that the Swedish Academy was right in stressing Naipaul's blurring of the boundaries between fiction and non-fiction. In many respects, Willie of *Half a Life,* for example, has character traits ascribable to Naipaul, and many figures elsewhere in his fiction. Emilienne Baneth-Nouailhetas argues in the same vein. The point of view of the narrator in the travel writings, she maintains, is much like Naipaul's own, expressed in articles and interviews. Through a detailed analysis of the comic and the humorous in Naipaul's travel writings she ably pinpoints the cultural position and ideology of the traveller and his condescending attitude towards the places and people he visits. Serafín Roldán-Santiago praises Naipaul's works, in particular *A Bend in the River*, for the fine use of caricature as a suitable form of social and political criticism, demonstrating at the same time the author's anti-colonial stance. Santiago's other essay "V.S. Naipaul's Vulcanization of Travel and Fiction

Paradigms" discusses how the fictional elements and travel paradigms of Naipaul fuse to give birth to a new, as yet indefinable, genre of literature. Pascal P. Buma reads Naipaul's *The Suffrage of Elvira* in the context of the genre of Bildungsroman. The article's narrow focus makes it an intensive study.

We believe the articles brought together in this anthology present a perceptive assessment of some of Naipaul's important works and his contribution to literature as a whole. We wish to thank all the contributors for their co-operation and K.R. Gupta of Atlantic Publishers and Distributors for suggesting the idea of this book in the first place.

—RAJESHWAR MITTAPALLI
—MICHAEL HENSEN

CONTENTS

1

Naipaul's Nobel

JOHN THIEME

Perhaps it shouldn't have done, but in many ways it came as something of a surprise to hear that V.S. Naipaul had won the 2001 Nobel Prize for Literature. His name had first been mentioned in connection with the Prize at least three decades before, at a time when his reputation was riding high with both the British literary establishment and in academic circles; and the succession of accolades that had been showered on him in the UK had culminated in the award of the Booker for *In a Free State* in 1971. At that time it seemed likely that, given the political rotations that appeared to characterize the award of the Nobel, there might well be a Caribbean winner and, if so, then surely Naipaul was a front runner. Then came the rumours that he *had* been short-listed, but rejected on the grounds that his work lacked sufficient humanitarian concern. They may have been unfounded, but the word was that the Nobel jury had been more sympathetic to the claims of Wilson Harris. There could be little doubt as to *his* humanitarian concern, but Harris, like Naipaul, was also to remain a bridesmaid in the ensuing years, allegedly nominated on several occasions but never finally finding favour with the jury.

When the Prize was awarded to Derek Walcott in 1992, it looked as though the door had been closed on both Naipaul and Harris. It seemed unlikely that another Anglophone

Caribbean writer would be in the frame for a generation or more. In the meantime, Naipaul's star had continued to ascend in certain spheres, while waning somewhat with academe. His American reputation had been established when *Guerrillas* (1975) was widely (mis?)read as an attack on black radicalism and consequently found favour as part of the backlash against 'sixties Black Power activism. And in the West more generally, as he increasingly turned from fiction to non-fiction, as well as producing works that conflated the two genres, his renown as an impartial observer of the malaise of postcolonial societies kept on growing and he was widely praised for a forthright clear-sightedness that provided an antidote to the shibboleths of political correctness. No matter that his supposed lucidity consigned whole continents and religions to oblivion, as he sweepingly declared that "Africa has no future"[1] and "Muslim fundamentalism has no intellectual substance to it, therefore it must collapse"[2] and in so doing played his own small part in widening the rifts between the world's 'haves' and 'have-nots'. No matter that from the outset he had dismissed his home island of Trinidad as "unimportant, uncreative, cynical,"[3] while allowing himself to be exempt from the charge of lack of creativity as a lone genius, who had heroically made a career for himself by escaping to the metropolis. No matter that he had dismissed the Caribbean as the "Third World's third world."[4] Naipaul's polemics served the needs of those among the Western intelligentsia who clung to the myth that there was a gaping chasm between 'them' and 'us', appeared to regret the demise of colonial 'order' and believed that the only solution to the problems of "the wretched of the earth" lay in the adoption of Western values. As they praised the perspicacity of his searing indictments of postcolonial societies, he, intentionally or otherwise, vicariously became their hatchet man. This, of course, says more about Naipaul's readers than the writer himself and, to be fair, his critique of non-Western societies as "half-made"[5] seems to have been born out of genuine conviction, but it still ministered to a metropolitan market for reactionary cultural commentary.

In any case, while Naipaul's writing continued to attract an increasing amount of adverse criticism outside the West, his popularity remained high in British establishments circles: he was knighted in 1990 and became the first winner of the David Cohen Prize for "lifetime achievement by a living British writer" in 1993. He had, after all, repudiated his Caribbean roots many years before and chosen to call himself a British writer. There were still numerous expressions of doubt about the writer's character: most notably in Paul Theroux's often acerbic account of his lengthy friendship with Naipaul, *Sir Vidia's Shadow*,[6] and also in books such as Diana Athill's *Stet*,[7] in which the author describes the apprehension she felt when dealing with VSN, as a senior editor at his long-time publisher, André Deutsch. Moreover, the level of interest in his work in Western academic circles declined as critics and students increasingly preferred the post-Rushdie generation of writers' stress on hybridity to Naipaul's emphasis on displacement. True, he could be seen as the forerunner of such writers, the literary scout who had disturbed monocultural assumptions many years before Rushdie, Ondaatje, Mo and others helped establish the migrant as the representative protagonist of the last quarter of the twentieth century, but then Walcott and Harris had both developed *their* nuanced accounts of the cross-cultural experience at much the same time as the early Naipaul and had done so without concessions to gesture politics or overt self-dramatization. Both Walcott and Harris were, and are, of course, 'difficult' authors, building metaphor into metaphor in their writing; and so perhaps it was not surprising that for many years they attracted less attention in this respect. Naipaul, in contrast, has worked in transparent modes, documenting concrete particulars in a spare style that appears to provide his readers with immediate access to actual situations rather than making them work their way through levels of interlocking imagery to find meaning. And perhaps it is the simple elegance of his prose style that has persuaded certain sections of his readership that he is a deft and discerning witness.

However, despite his brilliance in this vein, by the end of the last millennium it looked as though the Nobel should have passed Naipaul by. It seemed unlikely that there would be another Caribbean winner for the time being and in intellectual circles he was beginning to seem a yesterday's man, a writer whose penchant for pricking the bubble of political correctness had lost valency, as the debates moved on and became subtler. Despite the challenge to monoculturalism implicit in some aspects of his writing, he had from the first demonstrated a hostility to hybridity, for example in dramatizing a classically conservative attitude to the supposed perils of miscegenation in a novel such as *The Mimic Men* (1967). Given that Rushdie, Bhabha, Ondaatje, Ghosh and numerous other writers had pointed up the positive dimensions of migration and hybridity, Naipaul's nostalgic longing for a pure, Edenic moment in the past, when cultures were homogeneous,[8] seemed to be out of step with contemporary thinking about cultures, whether in the academy or, in this case, the world at large. Derek Walcott even found him provincial, when he located *The Enigma of Arrival* (1987) in the very English tradition of the "elegiac pastoralist."[9]

Some of the reductiveness and harshness of Naipaul's polemical attacks on postcolonial societies began to disappear. In *A Way in the World* (1994), he unearthed traces of the Amerindian cultures that underlay the Spanish foundations of Trinidad[10] and in so doing effectively overturned his earlier view of the island's past as centred on "the two moments when Trinidad was touched by history,"[11] two moments of contact with Europe; and he problematized issues of ancestral origins with a greater degree of humility than hitherto: "We cannot understand all the traits we have inherited. Sometimes we can be strangers to ourselves."[12] Slightly earlier, in *India: A Million Mutinies Now* (1990), he had taken a very different view of the sub-continent from that of his two previous books on India,[13] which had represented the country as irrevocably trapped in the quietism of a paralysing Hinduism that precluded Western self-realization and progress.[14] Now India was reconstructed as a mosaic of communal pieces, each asserting its distinctive capacity for creativity through "mutiny." Yet even this change left one uncomfortable, not so much because there was no real acknowledgement of the fairly total about-face he had taken, but because the book's evidence was assembled from a myriad of interviewees and, although most of it was written in inverted commas, the various interlocutors seemed to share a common sub-Naipaulian way of speaking. At the same time, Naipaul's public appeal continued to depend in part on his power as a gadfly. So, despite some evidence of a quieter, more humane Naipaul, if the criterion of humanitarianism remained important, he seemed an unlikely candidate for the Nobel as we entered the new Millennium.

However, other criteria were clearly at work. His name was still being mentioned and, after all, he had succeeded in reconstructing himself as British (while retaining the right to boldly comment where few Britons had commented before) and consequently the unlikelihood of there being another Caribbean laureate was not really relevant. So perhaps it should not have been a surprise to hear he had won the Prize. In any case, I'd like to speculate on why he may have found favour with the Nobel jury at this moment in time and also on whether he deserved the Prize. One thing that Naipaul has shared with Wilson Harris over the years is an extraordinary capacity to reinvent himself, while in a sense producing books that are all one work. Whether fiction or non-fiction, or an amalgam of the two, whether ostensibly about individuals or communities, this work is a continuing, often displaced, autobiography and Naipaul's more recent interviews have emphasized the highly personal nature of his writing. So much so that he now expresses surprise that he has touched a chord in other people, when his subject has been his own very particular experience. This is perhaps where his main achievement lies: in, consciously or unconsciously, having created a persona, with which, despite his testy polemics, we can identify all too readily. In his Nobel Lecture, he spoke of having "moved by intuition alone" without having any "guiding political idea,"[15] comparing himself with R.K. Narayan in this respect and identifying this lack of any overriding political conviction as an ancestral Indian trait. This involves a disturbingly stereotypical view of India, which again predicates an essentialist view of a particularly heterogeneous nation; and whether it is correct to characterize Narayan as he does presents a further difficulty, though at least it is endorsed by the creator of Malgudi's own habitual way of presenting himself—and certainly Narayan *is* less frequently and less overtly concerned with politics than Naipaul. But where Naipaul is concerned, it is extremely difficult to accept the writer at his own self-evaluation. In the Nobel Lecture, he intermingles autobiography with comments on phenomena such as "colonial shame and fantasy"[16] and one is left feeling—and again the author may be blissfully unaware of this—that the personal is highly charged with the political.

In his presentation speech at the Nobel ceremony, the Permanent Secretary of the Swedish Academy referred to Naipaul's having praised the West for recognizing "the right to individual endeavour" and for being devoted to European civilization as "the only one of the alternative cultures available to him that made it possible for him to become a writer."[17] In short, personal endeavour is possible in the West and not elsewhere—or at least this is so as far as Naipaul is concerned.

The Academy seems to have chosen him at this moment in time, because of his ostensible concern with the individual rather than the macro-political, without having grasped the extent to which his vision is suffused with politics and the extent to which his micro-politics embody a very particular pro-Western ideology. So could it be that it has arrived at a moment in its own evolution, when it wishes to distance itself from the charge that its decisions are influenced by political considerations, but has not appreciated just how politically charged Naipaul's writing is? Or, worse still, has it, in the wake of September 11th, fallen into line with America's declared war on the opponents of "freedom" and found a laureate who has frequently seen the West as the ultimate arbiter of freedom? If either of these speculations—and they are, of course, no more than speculations—has any substance, then the Academy has scored a spectacular own goal. In any case, Naipaul's expressed attitudes make it possible to imagine such a scenario.

Does Naipaul deserve the Prize? Individuals will have to decide for themselves. If a brilliant espousal of pro-Western conservative ideology and a revitalization of the tradition of pastoral elegy (the Academy's press release saw *The Enigma of Arrival* and not *A House for Mr Biswas* or *The Mimic Men* as his masterpiece[18]) are qualifications, then he surely does. And then there are his wonderfully pithy short sentences. To quote Derek Walcott's essay on *The Enigma of Arrival* once again, "There isn't a better English around, and for me this is wonderful without bewilderment, since our finest writer of the English sentence by praising the beauty of England, however threatened with industrial encroachment preserves it from itself."[19] Yet one doubts that prose style was at the top of the Nobel jury's shopping list when it came to choosing its 2001 laureate. Besides, Walcott's own sentences in this essay, and in many others, are at least as wonderful, albeit in a different vein; and so are those of a number of Naipaul's other contemporaries. The published citation does mention style, but puts more emphasis on other factors. The press release describes Naipaul as "a literary circumnavigator, only ever really at home in himself, in his inimitable voice" and refers to him as "[s]ingularly unaffected by literary fashion and models."[20] This suggests that it has taken Naipaul at his own estimate and in so doing succumbed to his self-perpetuated myth of himself as a lone genius who transcended his Caribbean origins.[21] The press release goes on to call him "a modern *philosophe,* carrying on the tradition that started originally with *Lettres persanes* and *Candide,*" saying that "he transforms rage into precision and allows events to speak with their own inherent irony."[22] The lack of awareness of the extent to which irony is culturally encoded and dependent on the agency of its author would be troubling in an undergraduate essay. Here it is more so, since it is compounded by the emphasis on Naipaul's adoption of Western values as the only means by which he could achieve fulfilment as a writer. There is a contradiction: on the one hand, Naipaul is a neutral witness, uninfluenced by cultural trends, who allows events to speak for themselves; on the other, he is a writer who has found himself through "his devotion to European civilisation" and its recognition of "the right to individual endeavour."[23] There appears to be a blindness to the extent to which Naipaul works within a Western discourse, which presents itself as unfashionable, but is in fact part of the conservative mainstream. The Academy's comments echo Naipaul's own numerous remarks on the failings of postcolonial societies, which of course are remarks that construct the irony that is supposedly inherent in events. In such a reading of world culture, individual endeavour has become the monopoly of the West, but Walcott, Harris and a million other mutineers suggest otherwise. Perhaps, then, it is best to make the case for Naipaul's Nobel in terms of his "wonderful" English sentences, but, as Walcott so astutely points out, they themselves are but the formal expression of his predilection for pastoral elegy.

Notes and References

1. "Meeting V.S. Naipaul," Naipaul interviewed by Elizabeth Hardwick, *New York Times Book Review* 13 May 1979: 36.
2. Naipaul interviewed by Edward Behr, *Newsweek* 18 Aug. 1980: 38.
3. V.S. Naipaul, *The Middle Passage* (1962; Harmondsworth: Penguin, 1969) 43.
4. V.S. Naipaul, *The Overcrowded Barracoon* (London: André Deutsch, 1972) 250.
5. E.g. in his essay "Conrad's Darkness" in *The Return of Eva Perón with The Killings in Trinidad* (London: André Deutsch, 1980) 216.
6. Paul Theroux, *Sir Vidia's Shadow: A Friendship across Five Continents* (Boston: Houghton Mifflin, 1998).
7. Diana Athill, *Stet* (London: Granta Books, 2000).
8. E.g. in the Epilogue to *In a Free State*: "[. . .] Perhaps that had been the only pure time, at the beginning, when the ancient artist, knowing no other land, had learned to look at his own and see it as complete," *In a Free State* (London: André Deutsch, 1971) 255.
9. Derek Walcott, "The Garden Path: V.S. Naipaul," *What the Twilight Says: Essays* (London: Faber, 1998): 122.
10. E.g. V.S. Naipaul, *A Way in the World* (London: Heinemann, 1994) 8, 41.
11. V.S. Naipaul, *The Loss of El Dorado* (1969; Harmondsworth: Penguin, 1973) 15.
12. V.S. Naipaul, *A Way in the World* (London: Heinemann, 1994) 9.
13. V.S. Naipaul, *An Area of Darkness* (London: André Deutsch, 1964); and *India: A Wounded Civilization* (London: André Deutsch, 1977.
14. See particularly *India: A Wounded Civilization* 25.
15. V.S. Naipaul, Nobel Lecture 7 Dec. 2001, Official Website of the Nobel Foundation <www.nobel.se/literature/laureates/2001/naipaul-lecture.html>.
16. Naipaul, Nobel Lecture.
17. Horace Engdahl, Presentation Speech: The 2001 Nobel Prize for Literature, Official Website of the Nobel Foundation <www.nobel.se/literature/laureates/2001/presentation-speech.html>.
18. Press Release, 11 Oct. 2001 <www.nobel.se/literature/laureates/2001/press.html>.
19. Walcott, "The Garden Path: V.S. Naipaul" 126.
20. Press Release, 11 Oct. 2000.

21. See Walcott, "The Garden Path: V.S. Naipaul" 127-28 on Naipaul's numerous predecessors and contemporaries who negate "The myth of Naipaul as a phenomenon, as a singular, contradictory genius who survived the cane fields and the bush at great cost [...]" 128.
22. Press Release, 11 Oct. 2000.
23. Engdahl, Presentation Speech.

2

The Novel of Migration

STUTI KHANNA

This paper proposes to analyse some recent novels which fall under the category of "novels of migration." I would like to look closely at the matrix of assumptions underlying the novels that constitute this category, as revealed by their formal and thematic concerns, and thereby try to enter into the conceptual grid that lies behind and dictates these assumptions. The analysis necessarily involves a close look at the figure of the migrant and the world(s) he sees himself as inhabiting. This leads to an attempt to locate the migrant within the poststructuralist/ postmodernist idiom, moving on to the politics of such location in the fiction these migrant writers write. I shall also trace the various forms the representation of the self / the protagonist in migrant writing has taken over the last few decades, and try to link those up with the changing literary as well as political concerns of this kind of writing.

The condition of migrancy is seen as a state of indeterminacy, of tentativeness, of "in-betweenness" as Homi Bhabha would call it. "The migrant is seen as the critical participant-observer into his/her own condition, enabling powerful insights to be made into the insider-outsider dichotomy and the real lived experiences of migration" (King et al xiii). He is defined by a "separation from origins and essences," a sense of "un-home-liness," occupying an indeterminate zone or "place of hybridity," leading to a necessary "creolisation" of identity (Bhabha 120). Diasporic thought has come to find its apotheosis in the ambivalent, transitory, culturally contaminated and borderline figure of the exile, caught in a historical limbo between home and the world. The very terms of reference to the condition of migrancy bring out its role in the legitimisation of 'otherness' in postmodernist discourse. As David Harvey writes, postmodernism is suspicious of meta-narratives, "abandoning the belief in universals," and stressing the "multiplicity and relativity of experiences" while also regarding "each strand as of potentially equal validity" (116). There is thus a strong relationship between the establishment of migrant or ethnic communities and the valourisation of the "other" in postmodernism. Iain Chambers has argued that migration, dislocation and ensuing marginality are some of the most important influences subverting long-standing beliefs in the linearity of progress and the stability of cultural identity, and that these have been determining influences on the inner conditions of contemporary humanity (King 6).

However, the concept of 'hybridity' and especially its celebration have pervaded migrant fiction only fairly recently. Postmodernism, basing itself largely on the work of Nietzsche, mounts an attack both on the idea of pure origins as well as the teleological view of world history And yet V.S. Naipaul, one of the first and greatest novelists of the Indian diaspora, creates a number of characters who are tormented by the unavailability of 'pure origins' to trace their descent from. The idea of an authentic and irreducible identity is intimately tied up with the possibility of achieving one's full potential in the "landscapes hymned by [one's] ancestors." However, history, or more specifically, the history of colonisation, has always undermined that dream of wholeness, leaving behind a "deep disorder" (*Mimic Men* 32), a legacy of cultural 'violation' and corruption. This leads, then, to a deep-rooted concern with the issues of mimicry and authenticity and assimilation that face a self caught on a cultural border.

Naipaul's position as a third generation Caribbean settled in England makes the idea of the return (to an unsullied past, and thereby a complete, rooted identity) doubly problematic. What past does one return to? Whose? The aboriginal peoples of the Caribbean have long been extinct. Most of its current inhabitants are descended from those brought there by slavery and indenture. Its languages took shape in the lands of the colonial masters, languages 'native' neither to the region nor to those who now speak them. In one of his essays, Naipaul wrote, "although the English language was mine [...] [its] tradition was not" (*Overcrowded Barracoon* 26). There is virtually no Caribbean 'tradition' that he can fall back upon, and this perhaps is the basis for his anguished sense of being not just a mimic writer, having to write in a tradition not his own, but also an inauthentic man. Anglicisation, or seeking to become a part of the country one has migrated to is, finally, in Bhabha's words, only a reminder that one is "almost the same but not quite [...] almost the same but not white" (86, 89).

Naipaul has also, in his many interviews and essays, made his own myth into that of the writer as a displaced person, one who does not "have a side, doesn't have a country, doesn't have a community; one [who] is entirely an individual," a figure who has achieved a Brahmanical "ideal of non-attachment" (*Overcrowded Barracoon* 16), a man without a home. His most well-known protagonist, Mr. Biswas sees 'manhood' as invariably linked to the ownership of "a house," a home, and therefore himself as not a man. One morning he says to his dog—"You are an animal and think that because I have a head and hands and look as I did yesterday I am a man. I am deceiving you. I am not whole" (*A House* 268). The self becomes inseparable from the house—to create the one is to achieve the other. Salim in *A Bend in the River* never sees his apartment as home, never even removes the stacks of bad paintings the previous owner has left behind her; "he keeps it as he found it, however inconvenient, as a permanent reminder that he has not made himself a place in the world and has therefore, as the novel's first sentence puts it, allowed himself 'to become nothing'" (Gorra 64).

An interesting feature about Naipaul's prose style has been noticed by commentators. The slow and stately rhythm of his prose, the measured tone, reflects a grim stolidity, and grants to it something of the status of fact. I shall have more to say about this aspect in a while. Here, I would like to conclude this brief discussion of Naipaul's work by highlighting the carefully controlled tension that marks it, the tension between his longing for an essential identity that constitutes specific groups and excludes others on the one hand, and his knowledge of the historical processes that always undermine such identities on the other. This leads Gorra to make generalised, universalist assumptions and statements:

> *A Bend in the River* uses the instability of Central African politics as the landscape against which to explore a world in which the past has been burnt away for everyone, in which humankind is everywhere homeless, so that the expatriate, estranged from the landscape his ancestors hymned, comes to stand as the representative figure of our time (160).

Most of the novels of migration that I have come across have had a first person narrative. The act of writing seems to become a sort of catharsis, as also a site for the creation/ exploration of the self, for the redefinitions of identity that necessarily take place with migration. Identity is increasingly seen as contingent and hermeneutically produced, as against something that is there, whole and present. First-person narration brings to the fore this idea of flux and fluidity associated with identity—and the act of writing becomes almost a means to work out one's sense of self. Memory is therefore invoked in a big way, since the past is revisited/reconstructed in an attempt to consolidate the present. Remembering, Bhabha writes, "is never a quiet act of introspection or retrospection. It is a painful re-membering, a putting together of the dismembered past to make sense of the trauma of the present" (63). This is borne out beautifully in the narratives of novels of migration. Memory fails to constitute a cohesive framework for the journey into the fractured past. The narratives of these novels are, in consequence, broken, discontinuous, fragmented. This fragmentation may manifest itself in different ways, but in each case, it demolishes the concept both of purity of origins and teleological progress. In Naipaul, this sense of fragmentation comes across not so much through the narrative style—which, in fact, as we saw above, actually counters it—as through the consciousness of the narrator, his deep and unshakable sense of loss, of being the perpetual outsider, the mimic man. Such a narrator destabilises any objectivity that the narrative may attempt to convey—the meditative, measured tone of the monologue is undercut by the fact of who is delivering it, which makes it profoundly disturbing. In Salman Rushdie's novels, on the other hand, the fragmentariness immediately hits the reader full in the face. It is a fragmentation both of form and content; moreover, a fragmentation that is delighted in and celebrated. He takes what Bhabha describes as that "separation from origins and essences" as his starting point. In attempting to define an independent India's "national longing for form" (*Midnight's Children* 291), he uses what he terms a "historically validated eclecticism" to mount an attack on "the confining myth of authenticity" itself (*Satanic Verses* 52). Saleem Sinai, the narrator in *Midnight's Children*, encompasses the whole of that India to which history has handcuffed him, not so much an individual as the choral voice of a national consciousness. The attempt to mirror the nation adequately then, calls for a heterogeneous, heteroglot, pluralistic narrative—a narrative that is bursting at the seams. It is here that Benedict Anderson's insistence upon the textual underpinnings of nation-ness is borne out. He sees nations as imaginative and cultural artifacts rather than empirical and scientific entities. They are imagined into coherence, and the novel and the newspaper become the two principal print forms capable of containing and representing, in one place, the impossible diversity that is the nation. Thus, the novel becomes a sort of proxy for the nation. Or, the other way of looking at it would be, as Alicja Cone says in *The Satanic Verses*, "Character isn't destiny any more. Economics is destiny. Ideology is destiny. Bombs are destiny" (432).

Compared with the restraint and almost classical purity of Naipaul's style, the one hallmark of Rushdie's teeming narrative is excess—sheer, unbridled excess. Necessarily, then, the claim to objectivity that Naipaul's prose makes is impossible in Rushdie's case. Rushdie, as a matter of fact, seems to have taken pains to highlight the unreliability of the narration in his novels, pointing on to the unreliability of all narration, of the very act of narrativisation. Further, he seems to have not only "reconciled" himself to "the inevitability" (*Shame* 69) of incompleteness and error, but actually revels in it. The final impression left by *Midnight's Children*, despite the bleak fate of the protagonist, is not bleak at all. The linguistic energy and improvisatory nature of the performance provides, in Rushdie's own words, "an optimistic counterweight to Saleem's personal tragedy" (*Imaginary Homelands* 16). As Gorra puts it so succinctly—"For the linguistic pluralism of the heteroglot novel is an ideological one as well, discrediting the belief that truth is one and absolute, and holding that it is instead multiple, overlapping, conflicting." He sees *A Bend in the River* as furnishing a negative example—its "monologic evenness of tone," its singular voice, is "frightening" in that it allows no escape from its narrator's despair (Gorra 121).

Again, if the hybridity of *Angrezi* marks the postcolonial "separation" of English from its "origins and essences," that same hybridity challenges any notion of an authentic Indian identity as well. Such a notion, as we have seen, is anathema to

Naipaul, for whom a fully autonomous identity can only be a dream of wholeness as long as the disabling knowledge of cultural 'violation' is present. Rushdie, on the other hand, claims to have "a plural identity [...] made up of bits and fragments from here, there" (qtd. in Marzorati 100). This recognition and acceptance of the self's unstable pluralism leads Rushdie on to the creative possibilities of mimicry, which he exploits to the utmost. Mimicry becomes more than Caliban's—"You taught me language, and my profit on't is, I know how to curse." Rather than being a mere oppositional strategy, it makes the very concept of binary oppositions redundant. As Bhabha puts it, such writing refuses to "oppose the pedagogy of the imperialist noun to the inflectional appropriation of the native voice," preferring instead "to go beyond such binaries of power in order to reorganise our sense of the process of identification in the negotiations of cultural politics" (Gandhi 153). Edward Said is also eloquent in his praise of the nomadic energies of migrant writers, whom he sees as transgressing the confinement of both imperial and provincial orthodoxies (Gandhi 153).

It is worthwhile, at this stage, to bring in Naipaul's notion of the "documentary heresy" ("The Documentary Heresy" 23). He argues that a simple record of the facts of pain and degradation is never enough. For such a record, he suggests, seems to acquiesce in that degradation by acknowledging one's powerlessness before it. The writer must instead accept his "interpretative function" and through that interpretation give us some way to comprehend experience. In other words, narrative becomes a means of meaning-making, of bringing about coherence, and thereby a means of resistance. And yet Naipaul's own novels, despite the strong narrativisation, do not convey any sense of meaningful resistance to the despair that threatens to swamp, and often does, the world of the novels—the overpowering impression that remains with the reader is that of a deep, unremitting bleakness.

Again, when one looks closer at the exhilarating possibilities that Rushdie's kind of polyglot, chutnified narrative throws up, one notices a rather disturbing phenomenon. Which is, that no matter how many varieties of linguistic hybridity its characters may embody, the language of the narratorial voice is almost always pure, unadulterated, classic English, and I use the term in the sense in which the writers of *The Empire Writes Back* do: establishment *English* as against local varieties of *english.* This observation leads one to disturbing inferences regarding the political stance that Rushdie embodies. Aijaz Ahmad raises similar questions, through his attack on the bewildering excess embodied in Rushdie's novels, so dazzling in its prodigiousness as to foreclose any possibility of action.

Ahmad takes as his starting point Rushdie's statements, in *Shame* and elsewhere, on the state of migrancy as a free-floating one, without a past or a history. As Rushdie puts it—"[...] we have come unstuck from more than land. We have floated upwards from history, from memory, from Time" (*Shame* 85). Ahmad's critique of Rushdie is on two counts. One is his valorization of his status as an exile. Ahmad quotes Raymond Williams to draw a distinction between exile and vagrancy—"there is usually a principle in exile, there is always only relaxation in vagrancy [...]" (157). Seeing the idea of "float[ing] upwards" as the most irresponsible form of vagrancy, Ahmad then goes on to question the replacement of the sense of loss which should follow rootlessness with that of celebration—"[...] the idea of belonging is itself seen now as bad faith, a mere '*myth* of origins'" (129). Secondly, Ahmad challenges Rushdie's reduction of the meaning of migration to a metaphorised plain, leading to his conclusion that "the migrant intellect roots itself in itself" (154), and the curious foreclosing of any kind of social or political engagement thereby, completing "the tie between social despair, a literal loss of reality, and narcissism" (155).

Ahmad's critique of the postmodernist notion of exile takes one back to one of the most influential embodiments of literary exile—James Joyce. Joyce left Ireland because he realised that he would be unable to fulfil his potential there—his first work, *Dubliners*, is a document of the inertia and claustrophobia Dublin evoked in him. Yet the decision to leave Dublin is a politically charged one, an act that is propelled by the desire to "forge the conscience of his race." Exile/migration, in his case, is a stance of involvement, a means of political enablement. In *Ulysses* we see the same Stephen, back in Ireland from France because of his mother's death, still agonising about what his Irishness means to him—he calls himself the "servant of two masters," English imperialism on the one hand and Irish, or Gaelic provincialism on the other. Again, the fragmented quality of the narrative of *Ulysses* also painstakingly creates, bit by bit, the town of Dublin—fragmentation becomes a means to build, to construct with greater authenticity what one has left behind. These elements of pain, of loss, coinciding with a deep political engagement with the homeland are rarely to be found in postmodernist migrant fiction. Leopold Bloom, despite the fragmented nature of the narrative, is not a patchwork creation the way Rushdie's Saleem is. There is a solidity to Bloom's character that neither Naipaul's nor Rushdie's protagonists seem to possess. The absence of involution and depth in the protagonists of their novels symptomises the attitudes of their creators. While Naipaul does not share the postmodernist "pleasures of unbelonging" (Ahmad 157), the bleakness of his novels is so absolute as to preclude any sense of political or personal enablement. Rushdie's stance, on the other hand, in which "belonging *nowhere* is nevertheless construed as the perennial pleasure of belonging everywhere" (157), is, in the last resort, a narcissistic, politically quietist stance.

After having placed the novel of migration, and discussed its distinctive features in the work of two important practioners, I would now like to turn to two recent works by two contemporary novelists, also from South Asia. These are *Funny Boy* by Shyam Selvadurai and *Tales from Firozsha Baag* by Rohinton Mistry. I have chosen these two novels for the striking similarities between them. While Mistry's work is explicitly a collection of intersecting tales, Selvadurai's novel has as its subtitle—"A novel in six stories." Both these works are semi-autobiographical, dealing with childhood, growing up and ultimately migrating—both, coincidentally, to Canada. What interests me in both these works is how the fact of migration affects both their formal as well as thematic concerns. The construction of the self, through the retrospective narrative of the authorial voice, becomes another interesting aspect in these novels.

Selvadurai's subtitling of his novel as a novel in six stories is interesting in the kind of fragmentation it symptomises. Fragmentation, as we saw above, is a narrative strategy that can be put to use in various different ways, to achieve widely different ends. The splitting up of a novel into six constituent parts, or conversely, as is the case with *Funny Boy*, the bringing together of separate stories to constitute a novel, seems to point to a mistrust of the very act of novel writing, of creating expansive, integrated, whole worlds in fiction. The only element linking these stories is the presence of Arjie, the narrator, and his experiences with various people, mark the process of his growing up. Arjie is, from the start, an outsider to the milieu he ostensibly is a part of. Each of the stories seems to follow a set pattern—Arjie is caught between two opposing worlds, or world-views, and chooses to belong to one. By the end of the chapter, he realises that he cannot belong there any longer, and finds himself stranded, as it were. The story entitled "Pigs can't Fly" lays out such divisions at the very outset—"Territorially, the area around my grandparents' house was divided into two" (*Funny Boy* 3)—the "front garden," which "belonged to the boys," and the "back garden," the "territory of the girls." Arjie finds himself, paradoxically enough, "gravitat[ing] naturally" towards the girls. In that world, to which he cannot and yet does belong naturally, he is "able to leave the constraints of [his]self and ascend into another, more brilliant, more beautiful self" (4).

This self-gratification is, however, short-lived—he begins to be seen as "funny" (14), as a "girlie-boy" (25). A quarrel with the girls makes him realise that their world is lost to him forever: "I would be caught between the boys' and the girls' worlds, not belonging or wanted in either" (39). What Arjie voices so poignantly here is what Bhabha says about the migrant—the fact of his inhabiting an interstitial, liminal zone, on the margins of two worlds, belonging to neither.

Even more interesting than this is what the narrator says, from his vantage point of the present, about his childhood:

> Yet those Sundays, when I was seven, marked the beginning of my exile from the world I loved. Like a ship that leaves a port for the vast expanse of the sea, those much looked forward to days took me away from the safe harbour of childhood towards the precarious waters of adult life (5).

A statement like this seeks to inject the sense of exile into life as a whole; it implies that the very process of growing up is an exile—an exile from one's former, younger self. Exile seems to have become a condition of existence, a universal ontological state, from which there is no way out.

The subsequent chapters/stories re-enact, in different ways, the same pattern of loss. The growing closeness Arjie attains with both Radha Aunty and Daryl Uncle, which comes to an abrupt end in both cases, only reinforces the pervasive sense of loss that marks the narratorial consciousness. "We would return to a regular routine, yet nothing could take us back to where we had been before the day I looked up from my book and saw Daryl Uncle at the gate" (153). It is worth remarking that even a mentioning of emigration is made for the first time only on page 195 of the book, by Arjie's mother, fearful of the political tumult around them. And yet, the narrator's sense of migration, of exile, pervades the novel from the very outset. His homosexuality becomes another marker of difference, and thereby of non-belonging.

This sense is reinforced in Victoria Academy, the new school Arjie is sent to in an attempt to make him part of the boys' world. The Tamil-Sinhalese conflict in Sri Lanka is mirrored there in the shape of the rivalry between "Black Tie" and Lokubandara. It is here that Arjie experiences politics at close quarters—politics that has insinuated itself into bathroom brawls between boys and poems for children. His Tamil identity in no way makes his choices clearer for him:

> I was not sure that, as a Tamil, my loyalties lay with Black Tie. I thought of Mr. Lokubandara and the way Salgado and his friends had assaulted that Tamil boy. I thought of the way Black Tie had beaten both Shehan and me. Was one better than the other? I didn't think so. Although I did not like what Mr. Lokubandara stood for, at the same time I felt that Black Tie was no better (247).

Again, he is caught in an impasse, in-between two worlds, not belonging in either. His apathy towards politics or political divisions does not immunise him from its insidious effects, however—his realisation of the fact that his friend and lover, Shehan, is a Sinhalese draws "a thin, translucent screen" (302) between them. Paradoxically, the relationship with Shehan also draws him away from his family—"I was no longer a part of my family in the same way. I now inhabited a world they didn't understand and into which they couldn't follow me" (285). His statement expressing relief, then, towards the end of the novel, at migrating to Canada—"[...] I long to be out of this country. I don't feel at home in Sri Lanka any longer [...] " (304) is almost redundant. He has never felt at home at any stage of his life; the novel is a testimony to his sense of being the perennial outsider, the eternal exile.

Rohinton Mistry's *Tales from Firozsha Baag*, like *Funny Boy*, takes a stance vis-à-vis the well-made novel Mistry painstakingly pieces together, bit by bit, an entire world in minute detail: *Firozsha Baag* seems to me to be comparable to *Ulysses* in the brilliant, pulsatingly alive presentation of a tiny world. And yet Mistry chooses *not* to give that world the coherence that a novel would give it—a task not beyond his capacity, as his other brilliant works of fiction tell us. The fragmentation, then, has a point, and it seems to be to reinforce the sense of being "not whole" that is incumbent upon every migrant (writer).

Parsis have an ancient history of migrancy—they came to India from Persia because of Islamic persecution in the seventh century, and stayed on ever since, both as part of the land of migration, and yet not wholly so. The world of *Firozsha Baag,* in its very cloisteredness, highlights this sense of difference with which the Parsis view themselves. The first story in the collection, "Auspicious Occasion," begins with a defiant, almost aggressive positing of markers of difference—terms unfamiliar even to 'the average Indian' are thrust upon the reader thick and fast—*Behram roje, dugli, pheytoe,* etc. The world outside Firozsha Baag is seen as populated, swarming, with *ghatis.* As Kersi, the young boy who narrates three of the stories in the collection, and whose life threads through the book, says—"In the particular version of reality we inherited, *ghatis* were always flooding places, they never just went there" (176). Mistry brings out with great skill both the sense of persecution assailing a small community, getting smaller by the day, tenaciously holding on to its identity, as well as the claustrophobia such incestuousness can breed, especially in stories such as "Condolence Visit," or the vicious violence that can erupt in a small, ordinarily peaceful community—as in "One Sunday." This story also introduces us to our protagonist, Kersi, who stands out from the rest of his people by the sensitivity of his reaction to the vicious community assault on Francis, a young wastrel, for having stolen a paltry sum of money. Kersi appears again as the narrator of the beautiful "Of White Hairs and Cricket" where, overtaken by nostalgia, he muses:

> It had been such a long time since we last played cricket. Flying kites had also become a thing of the past. One by one, the things I held dear were leaving my life, I thought gloomily. And Francis. What about poor Francis? Where was he now [...]? (115)

One notices here the same sense of loss that had plagued Arjie at every stage of his life—the inevitable loss caused by the passing of time. The story then movingly goes on to reinforce this:

> I felt like crying [...] for *Mamaiji* and her tired, darkened eyes spinning thread for our *kustis*, and for Mummy growing old in the dingy kitchen [...] I wanted to weep for myself, for not being able to hug Daddy when I wanted to, and for not ever saying thank you [...] and for all the white hairs that I was powerless to stop (120).

Loss, then, becomes integral to the fact of being human—one is *born* a migrant.

"Squatter" talks about the fate of the migrant in a foreign land in a comic-tragic vein. Sarosh is unable to adjust to life in a foreign country, even after trying for as long as ten years, and eventually has to return. The "land of milk and honey" is only "a pain in the posterior" for him. However, back home, "the old pattern was never found by Sarosh; he searched in vain. Patterns of life are selfish and unforgiving" (167). Again, he is the classic case of the in-between man, a human void.

Kersi, when he migrates to Canada, like his author has, sees himself as "someone out of a Greek tragedy, guilty of the sin of hubris for seeking emigration out of the land of [his] birth [...]. I, Tiresias, blind and throbbing between two lives, the one in Bombay and the other to come in Toronto [...]" (180). In "Swimming Lessons," Kersi tries to learn how to swim when he is in Canada, and fails. If swimming is a metaphor for control, the story conveys Kersi's sense of helplessness in a foreign country. He, however, writes. In a self-reflexive vein, Mistry talks about Kersi's writing as that "of an immigrant, it provides a different viewpoint; the only danger is if he changes and becomes so much like them that he will write like one of them and lose the important difference" (248).

What is this "important difference?" How does it make itself known? More importantly, what does the articulation of this difference achieve? This question seems to me to be the crux of the matter. This paper has traced the various ways in which some of the significant migrant writers have perceived and presented this sense of difference. The crucial question, however, is whether this knowledge of their difference has led to any kind of enablement. Can the only responses to this in-between status be a narcissistic *joie-de-vivre*, or a numbing bleakness, or plain confusion, as seems to be the case with the two novelists we have just discussed. Can this *hybridised* identity bring about some kind of meaningful socio-political engagement? This, I think, is the task the novel of migration needs to address itself to.

Works Cited

Ahmad, Aijaz. *In Theory: Classes, Nations, Literatures.* London: Verso, 1992.

Anderson, Benedict. *Imagined Communities: Reflections on the Origin and Spread of Nationalism.* 1983. London and New York: Verso, 1991.

Bhabha, Homi. *The Location of Culture.* London: Routledge, 1994.

Gandhi, Leela. *Postcolonial Theory: A Critical Introduction.* New Delhi: OUP, 1999.

Gorra, Michael. *After Empire: Scott, Naipaul, Rushdie.* Chicago: U of Chicago P, 1997.

Harvey, David. *The Condition of Postmodernity.* Oxford: Basil Blackwell, 1989.

King, Russell, John Connell and Paul White, eds. *Writing Across Worlds: Literature and Migration.* London: Routledge, 1995.

Marzorati, Gerald. "Salman Rushdie: Fiction's Embattled Infidel." *New York Times Magazine* 29 Jan. 1989.

Mistry, Rohinton. *Tales from Firozsha Baag.* Toronto: Penguin Books, 1987.

Naipaul, V.S. *The Mimic Men.* 1967. Harmondsworth: Penguin, 1969.

——. *The Overcrowded Barracoon.* 1972. New York: Vintage, 1984.

——. *A House for Mr. Biswas.* 1961. New York: Vintage, 1983.

——. "The Documentary Heresy." *Critical Perspectives on V.S. Naipaul.* Ed. Robert D. Hamner. London: Heinemann, 1979.

Rushdie, Salman. *Midnight's Children.* New York: Knopf, 1981.

——. *The Satanic Verses.* New York: Viking, 1989.

——. *Shame.* London: Jonathan Cape, 1983.

——. *Imaginary Homelands.* New Delhi: Penguin Books, 1991.

Selvadurai, Shyam. *Funny Boy: A Novel in Six Stories.* New Delhi: Penguin Books, 1994.

3

The Politics of Fluidity in *A Bend in the River*

FAUSTO CIOMPI

A Bend in the River is probably Naipaul's highest and most convincing pronouncement on modern Africa and, more generally, on the uncertain possibility of politically transforming the third world. It is also a study of the threats levelled against individual integrity by selfishness, political tyranny and racial uprootedness. But the novel's thematic range is far more extended and complex than stated above. *A Bend in the River* thematizes, in fact, such challenging issues as the clash of ancestral traditions with modernization; the tragi-comic exercise of tyranny in the form of the exasperated cult of personality, which reduces the citizens of Africa to puppets in the hands of a capricious ruler; the corruption and arbitrariness of the army, the administrators, policemen, bureaucrats, who live, however, in the unnerving expectation of the dictator's cruel and unpredictable decisions; the varied responses of the diverse races and cultures to the African landscape, climate and politics (Indians, Europeans, natives from the bush, half-castes, Africans of Hindu origin); the ineffectual and sometimes ridiculous political role of European intellectuals, who, as unconscious *instrumenti regni*, pathetically herald all the shifts in direction in the President's politics, all his whims and follies, as illuminated moves of unprecedented cultural consequence; the sham of African modernization, which turns the continent into a pallid echo of Europe: this modernization process produces neither commodity nor services. Indeed, its primary objective is that of satisfying the President's ambitions and, incidentally, tickling the people's fetishistic love for the machine, the archaic symbol of proto-industrialism.

In such a political context, individuals struggle on their way to self-realization, strutting and fretting their hour of love, social ambition or vainly sought-for human accomplishment invariably with little or no success. The novel opens with a fatalistic assessment of failure as the likeliest outcome for those who are unable, in Nietzschean terms, to forge their destiny by the hammer of their will: "The World is what it is; men who are nothing, who allow themselves to become nothing, have no place in it"[1] (9). It is a note that will be gloomily struck again in the story as an assertion of the meaninglessness of man's efforts to change his position in the world (21). In the conflict between social context and individual effort, the world invariably prevails: "We had become what the world outside had made us; we had to live in the world as it existed" (252).

Indeed, Salim's town has undergone epochal changes, which are duly recorded by the narrator in the final part of the text:

> Forest at a bend in the river, a meeting place, an Arab settlement, a European outpost, a European suburb, a ruin like the ruin of a dead civilization, the glittering Domain of new Africa, and now this [the kingdom of horror determined by the politics of "radicalization" and tyranny] (269).

The town at the bend in the river has experienced the rise and decline of more than one civilization: local people feel like ghosts from the future, as though their life had already been lived out and now they were looking at its relics: "You were in a place where the future had come and gone" (33). Consequently, they seem indifferent to the chaotic events of macrohistory and, as they observe life and politics with apparent fatalism, they are oblivious to everything that does not concern their personal safety or private business. Despite the dramatic historical changes, a sense of psychological immutability pervades people's life and language, as is shown by the frequent tautologies and emphatic semasiological figures which describe personal and social experience as a vicious circle: "I knew only what I knew" (47); "I am the kind of person I am [. . .]" (48); "the law was what it was [. . .]" (198); "Copper was copper [. . .]" (207); "The past was simply the past" (17). The stasis and circularity of this kind of existence are clearly expressed by the following sentence, in which epanadiplosis, or the iteration of "there" at the beginning and at the end of the sentence, confirms the immutability of Mahesh's and Shoba's life after a series of sanguinary historical vicissitudes: "There was no change there" (267). Life is as meaningless and half-nonsensical as a dream: "It seemed to me that men were born only to acquire experience; the quality of the experience was immaterial; pleasure and pain—and, above all, pain—had no meaning; to possess pain was as meaningless as to chase pleasure" (229).

Salim intends to reject his people's timeless fatalism and pursue individual achievement in society without being involved in history and politics. He belongs to a people without past, without history: "History was something dead and gone, part of the world of our grandfathers, and we didn't pay too much attention to it" (186). What he knows comes from books written by Europeans: his historical knowledge is based on postcolonial mediation or cultural fabrication. As Michael Gorra (98-99) has argued, Salim should have been a more careful interpreter of inscriptions:

> When he first arrives at the bend in the river, Salim finds a ruined monument inscribed with a Latin tag: *Miscerique probat populos et foedera jungi.* The ruins are those of a memorial the colonial steamship company erected to celebrate itself, and the words mean the gods approve of the mixing of the continents and the peoples. The wreckage unnerves him—"the steamer monument had been knocked down," an attempt "to wipe out the memory of the intruder"—but the sentiment makes him hopeful (26). Only

> the quotation is wrong, a mistake that prefigures his own later illusions about his affair with Yvette. For it's drawn from Book IV of the *Aeneid*, where the gods emphatically do not approve—and in consequence Dido perishes. When Salim learns the truth he both marvels at and is appalled by the way the imperial powers have manipulated the past in the service of their rule. It means that the city is based on a lie, a kind of lie that would later build the New Domain—a misquotation that paradoxically confirms the opposition it attempts to deny.

If Indar, Salim's intellectual friend, theorizes the necessity to "trample on the past" (120) and to make a fresh start in self-realization through cultural development and cosmopolitanism, Salim, instead, makes the same journey as the slaves had made in reverse: from the east coast to central Africa. His journey towards the heart of the continent is, then, also a journey to the heart of Africanness and the essence of slavery. But his confrontation with racial alterity, personified especially by Zabeth the magician, leaves him quite unresponsive and indifferent. Indeed the 'other,' to Salim, is outside himself and the experience of dissociation of personality and estrangement which he makes in the forest is of no great consequence: "you heard yourself as though you were another person" (14). The true otherness Salim will have to discover concerns the other as social and historical being, so that he will be obliged to abandon the middle ground between absorption in life and aloofness he has chosen to occupy. Salim feels "unprotected, an intruder" (14) in the forest, but the river appeases him and brings him back to something outside time, something eternal: "to what was there a hundred years ago, to what had been there always" (14), "the eternal noise at that bend in the river" (75). But if occasionally, in the first part of the story, the river represents the call of timelessness, ultimately, it embodies the flow of history which takes away with itself Salim and the Africans, the would-be observers of the historical tragedy along with the victims of political violence.

The stylistics of *correctio* and epiphrasis: plot, structure and narrative voice

In broad outline, the novel, which is almost entirely set in an unnamed African country in large measure modelled on Mobutu's Zaire, tells the story of Salim, an Indian-born merchant from a coastal town who abandons the fatalistic and sedentary customs of his people and decides to try his fortune as a shop-dealer in an unnamed place at the bend in a river, somewhere in central Africa. There Salim does reasonably good business, has an affair with Yvette, the wife of a French historian (Raymond, who is at the service of the country's president), and lives out his monotonous life in the midst of the continuous political turmoil caused by the Big Man in power (obviously, the fact that both the President and his country are unnamed makes them the representatives of Africa as a whole and all African dictators). Following his break with Yvette, Salim moves to London; here he tries to make a new life for himself and considers the opportunity of marrying Kareisha, the girl who had been promised to him since he was a child. But in London he feels uprooted and useless. Consequently, he resolves to go back to the town at the bend in the river, but there he finds out that nationalization has deprived him of his shop, where he is reduced to working as an employee. Salim starts smuggling ivory and gold but is soon discovered and imprisoned. He faces torture and probable death except that he is saved by an officer, Ferdinand, a former student of the town lycée and a friend of Metty's, Salim's servant. Salim is thus allowed to leave the town secretely on a steamer which, while journeying up the river, is assaulted by people who are probably fleeing the country themselves, because they have been terrorized by the President's escalation of horrors. The assault is repelled, and Salim continues his goalless journey away from Africa.

The novel is divided into four parts, whose titles are clearly concerned with political life: The Second Rebellion (the Big Man's accession to power), The New Domain (the cultural innovations in the European style introduced by the President), The Big Man (the progressive reduction of the exercise of power to absurd tyranny), Battle (the assault on the steamer on which Salim is leaving Africa probably carried out by people in flight from the country). Furthermore, despite the lack of inadequacy between the chapter titles and the events actually narrated, it must be underlined that the macroevents of the political sphere—reverberating like dreadful echoes from the capital to the province—are foregrounded especially when they interfere with Salim's life.

Primarily the story is told in the first person by Salim, that is, in narratological terms, by a homodiegetic-autodiegetic narrator, who is not just a narrative voice but the protagonist of the story he is telling. The received idea that an I-narrator tends to bias the reader in favour of the narrator-character is not disconfirmed by this novel. Indeed, Salim seems to be a reliable narrator whose attitude to reality is inspired by matter-of-fact-realism. He is perfectly aware of the prejudices he has inherited from his race. His unpretentious account of complex political issues is more effective in that it is indirect: he rejects or ignores all ideologies and reacts to them with indifference, irony or wise scepticism; nonetheless, he experiences their absurd effects in his private life of would-be detached observer of the world. His rendering of the political events does not impoverish their significance: he can look at the world around himself without simplifying it too much. The status of observer is granted to Salim by his birth and aim in life: he is not African, neither a visitor nor a settler, but simply someone with no better place to go. As an outsider, to an extent, he is thus allowed to observe the violence around him from a separate standpoint: "I was neutral [...] I wanted the old balance to be maintained" (74); "In my own mind I separated myself from them. I still thought of myself as a man passing through" (102).

But Salim's is not the only narrative voice in the novel. Other characters occasionally perform the function of narrator, especially when they recall analeptically long episodes from their existence in non-African contexts. This is the case with Indar's account of his stays in London (the starting point of a promising career as lecturer and cultural promoter), and in New York (where he touches the nadir of his fortune); or Shoba's report of her journey to India culminating in the disfigurement of her face: an incident that, in her view, makes the malediction her family threw on her for marrying Mahesh come true; or also Yvette's narration of her days with Raymond, in Europe or in the capital of the unnamed African country they move to. These usually long inserts take the form of long soliloquies which transform Salim from narrator or interlocutor involved in the dialogic exchange into a silent addressee. They are structurally needed to cover events outside Salim's limited range of experience and beyond his necessarily incomplete knowledge of other characters' lives and motivations. But if the story line does not usually depart from what the I-narrator is thinking, doing or witnessing, it is not only due to the obvious limits inherent in homodiegeticity. Narration always focuses on Salim or on his interlocutors and interactants because Naipaul wants to instil into the reader the impression of living in the perennial present of Salim's life. The narrative act is performed by one who freely admits he belongs to a people that lives as if between past and present there were no break: "there was always only the present. It was as though, as a result of some disturbance in the heavens, the early morning light was always receding into the darkness, and men lived in a perpetual dawn" (18-19). Accordingly, Salim narrates the events that take place in the novel in a more or less chronological sequence, which reflects the order of his day by day experiences. He lives in a perennial present, taking in what is at hand and ready to be shaped into a narrative; he does not pay attention to the events occurring in the outer world until they enter the sphere of his experience: the dimension of simultaneity is almost completely excluded from his narrative act. We know little, for instance, about Indar when his presence on stage is not required in order to illustrate

Salim's condition either by contrast (at the beginning and in the central part of the story, when the enterprising Indar seems to be on the winning side and Salim is instead the inert continuator of long-established racial habits) or by analogy (at the end of the story, when Indar too experiences failure). Indar's presence in the story, like that of Nazruddin, is governed by an inflexible narrative logic which needs *exempla* to make an axiological or political point clear. And the succession of narrative frames thematically organized around a central idea or episode is the structural outcome of such a continuity in narration.

Continuity, or at least connection, is also evident in the novel's most striking stylistic feature, which is the independent or combined occurrence of short sentences starting with "and" or "but." This stylistic trait recurs in other novels by Naipaul, and its meaning and function vary according to the semantic cotext or by the archiseme (i.e. the sense-dominant lexical and conceptual unit) that encompass and determine the text's semantics. In *A Bend in the River*, the alternation of incipital coordinate and adversative clauses state or mime the instability of individual existence and socio-political life, a consequence of which is the need to re-define one's position continuously within the changing context. Here are some instances that regard the combined and juxtaposed use of sentences starting with "and" or "but":

> BUT the taxis stank of disinfectant; the officials of our health department were fierce about taxis. AND for this reason (95).
>
> BUT for some reason—Mahesh might have told him he was being watched—he never troubled Mahesh again. AND not long afterwards he was posted away from our town (102).
>
> 'AND now you do this.' I was acting. BUT there are times when we act out what we really feel, times when we cannot cope with certain emotions, and it is easier to act. AND Metty was acting too [. . .] (113).

AND we had considered them parasites and half dangerous, serving some hidden cause of the President's, people we had to be careful with. BUT now, being with them in the Domain [. . .] (124).
AND of course in those days Africa wasn't a subject. BUT I never made a secret of what I felt or where I stood, and suppose the word must have got around (138).
BUT then Yvette, straightening up, and remembering to smile, said to me 'Are you seeing someone off too?' AND I understood that my anxiety was foolish (169).
BUT I didn't know about Europeans and their restaurant habits. AND the Tivoli was meant for our Europeans (174).
AND my fear was at once the fear of failing with her, being left with nothing, and the fear of the consequences of success. BUT that alarm vanished the next afternoon when she came to the flat (179).
BUT that was what I had now. AND it wasn't open to me to withdraw (191).
AND I was expecting to get some indirect word. BUT in all these months he hasn't even sent me his regards (195).
BUT Raymond showed no uncertainty. AND he was loyal [. . .] (198).
BUT now secrecy wasn't possible and didn't seem to matter. AND we never worried about Metty in the flat again (200).
BUT Yvette was restless. AND that was a bad sign for me (204).
AND I used to think of him as a fellow survivor! BUT it wasn't for me to condemn him or others (208).
BUT we mustn't get pissed too soon; he had something to say to us. AND it was known that the statement the President was going to make was about our Youth Guard (214).
AND it could easily have ended as a shouting match, no more. BUT the officer had stumbled and fallen. BUT nothing had happened. Everyone had been waiting to see what the President would do. BUT for more than a fortnight the

President had said and done nothing. AND what the President said now was staggering (215).

BUT there had been no leaflets then, no leaders as young and educated as these. AND there was something else (220).

BUT then she said, 'Raymond will want to make love to me when he sees me looking like this.' AND that was unusual, not like her at all (224).

BUT it had been taken as settled from the start. AND, really, it was comforting [. . .] (239).

BUT Metty didn't come down. AND all that he said when I went up the external staircase [. . .] (263).

BUT then he changed his mind and went to the store-room, his office. AND I left, to go and look for Mahesh at Bigburger (266).

BUT there was no plan; there was no law; this was only make-believe, play, a waste of men's time in the world. AND how often here, even in the days of bush [. . .] (277).

BUT this was all that the jail—on the part of it I was in—was about. AND it was awful (278).

BUT nobody knows what is going to happen. AND the President is smart (284).

It must be observed, however, that the incipital "but" or "yet," just like the initial "and," occur much more frequently than suggested by the instances above. To provide a random but significant documentation, it can be noted that on pages 94 and 195, eleven sentences are opened either by BUT or by AND; on page 187 five consecutive sentences begin with YET (four times) or BUT (once). On pages 197-99 no less than fourteen sentences contain the initial linkers. Page 212, just like pages 198 and 285, has six occurrences; pages 99 and 224 contain seven instances each; page 249 has eight; page 161 has nine, and so on.

The use of "and" often generates the figure of epiphrasis resulting in the unexpected adjunct of information. The use of "but" combined with "not" generates the rhetorical figures of *correctio* or *distinctio*, as in the following examples:

> AND then the pressure eased. NOT because the President acted, as I had been hoping. BUT because violence had come to our town. NOT the evening drama of street brawls and murders, BUT a steady, nightly assault in different areas, AND police stations AND officials AND official buildings (218).

> AND you remember how he used to get on. NOT talking about money, BUT it was always there. You would say that he felt that money had made him holy. All rich people are like that, I suppose. AND that was one idea about himself that Indar never lost. His outfit DIDN'T give him back his money BUT it made him holy again (249).

The characters and the narrator use these figures with the purpose of continuously correcting or re-defininining the meaning or illocutionary force of their speech acts. Their anxiety to re-open a sentence that had been closed, their incessant need to provide specifics, to consider alternatives, to make things clear as if they desired to justify themselves before an inflexible authority are symptoms of enslavement to political and psychological forces that have been interiorized and proffer continuously new and ungraspable models of behaviour and thinking. Hermeneutic and existential uncertainty are expressed by the incessant need to conform to the new politics and philosophy imposed by the President. Reality is made incongruous and puzzling by permanent change, and its significance becomes progressively absurd. The order initially established by the Big Man, cruel but clear and felt by the people as imposed by a gruesome and overseeing intelligence, is replaced by chaos and corruption caused by the ludicrous and absurd exercise of the cult of personality. The Big Man's policies are effective because he is everything: extremes meet in his person. The President's policies oscillate between exasperated modernization and return to the bush, between socialist egalitarianism and tyrannical arbitrariness, between the worship of an ancestral and maternal Black Madonna and modern ideas on woman's liberation. He is the guardian of tradition and the audacious innovator. He resorts to the iconic language of larger-than-life portraits hanging everywhere in the country and to the various linguistic registers or forms of degraded instrumentalism of language, which he adopts for the sake of permanent propaganda (the official language of historians and journalists, the directness of short maxims and catchwords, the language of high European culture, the monkey language of the bush, the vulgar language of the gutter), until the tyrant finds drama a more suitable means of expressing himself and decides to enact his pathological exercise of power as a sadistic theatrical rite. This happens when the President's officers are summoned to a meeting which will end with the execution of one of them, still ignorant of his fate.

The language of power is a cunningly woven mesh of complexity and brutality, whose outstanding features are metamorphosis and unpredictability. Epiphrasis, *correctio, distinctio* are the poor rhetorical strategies most frequently adopted by people when they defend themselves from incessant political and existential change, as well as by the arbitrariness of authority and of fate. The syntactical pattern established by an initial "and" or "but" is, then, also the equivalent of the psychological and political fluidity foregrounded in the novel: phrases, just like experience, are not absolute and self-contained, they must often be re-opened up and revised. In Foucaultian terms, self-governance is just as impossible as maintaining the *polis*, that is, the government of the others in a rationally organized community. The Platonic homology between the political structure and the structure of the self, both deranged and endangered, is asserted (Foucault 71).

The ethics of survival: to carry on in historical fluidity

Salim's family is Muslim, but they are a special group who feels close to the Hindus of north-western India, from where they originally come. Salim describes them as deprived of history; for them, life is an eternal present: "We simply lived; we did what was expected of us, what we had seen the previous generation do. We never asked why; we never recorded [. . .] the past was simply the past" (17) and "We continued to live as we had always done, blindly" (23). This lack of perspective makes them concerned with what is spatially close and what is chronologically immediate. But this a-historical fatalism also affects Salim, Mahesh and most people from the town at the bend in the river, as is clearly revealed by their frequent use of verbs like "carry on" and "keep on," which express the intention to indefinitely extend the present that Salim and people like him are living. On the other hand, the here and now that Salim experiences is to be continuously reconsidered in view of the President's unpredictable and capricious decisions. It is a day-by-day politics or ethics of survival which does not regard only ordinary people like Salim or Mahesh, but the intellectuals too. This is Raymond speaking: "We have no idea where the continent is going. We can only carry on" (143) and "We must carry on" (78), says Mahesh after the Big Man's accession to power. A philosophy which is easily accepted by most people in the town: "We did only what we could do. We followed Mahesh's motto: we carried on" (104). To Salim, business is "a way of carrying on, and a way of passing the time" (81). In time, he loses the faculty of action: "And, forgetting goals, I kept on, living my life [. . .]" (221). While Father Huismans, the European teacher at the local lycée and collector of African art items, feels part of a great historical process (the "immense flow of history" [68] that could not be disturbed by his own death), natives and settlers in Salim's town think their death would be equally irrelevant just because they know anything they do may go to waste at any moment. They are aware they are "expendable" (94), but, despite their precariousness, they cling to their daily activities: "But we were like the ants; we kept on" (94) and "In fact, the less educated we were, the more at peace we were, the more easily we were carried along by our civilization or civilizations" (59). In the wake of all the political changes and of the most sanguinary events or explosions of political madness, the basic attitude of the people stays the same: "Africa was a place where we had to survive" (126). Individuals go through all the changes in macrohistory with the illusion of continuity, but their life is far from being full and meaningful. This is Salim's brooding on the end of his affair with Yvette: "But that idea of continuity, however overpowering at those intimate, narrow moments, was an illusion, as I knew" (223). Life, just like history, is a shapeless flow whose continuous metamorphosis prevent people from calling 'home' the place where they live, or 'wife' the occasional lover—frequently, a prostitute—they spend some time with. Africa is no place to build, or to settle. To Salim, it is a very special sort of home: "Africa was my home [. . .]" (17); "But home was hardly a place I could return to. Home was something in my head" (114). Africa is a place to think of when experiencing displacement and uprootedness in Europe, at least for enjoying the "comfort of 'going back' [. . .] of perhaps, not having, after all, to be here" (240). It is a reassuring idea which supplements the subject's self-opacity, his incapacity to read within himself, and his inability to feel at home anywhere in the world. Naipaul demystifies both the Nietzschean and postmodernist ethics of living daringly and groundlessly by squandering oneself in the world, and, at the same time, the pre-political view that home may be an idealized free zone outside history. These views are clearly envisaged as a matter of inauthenticity:

> The idea of going home, of leaving, the idea of the other place—I had lived with it in various forms for many years. In Africa it had always been with me. In London, in my hotel room, I had allowed it on some nights to take me over. It was a deception. I saw now that it comforted only to weaken and destroy (252).

What the myth of "the other place" conceals is the ripping of the personal accomplishment from public responsibility. One dreams of a ready-made paradise, or such a sedate milieu as that of a town at the bend in a river, where one can settle and cultivate inwardness; but then one wakes up to a political nightmare that contaminates the private sphere of experience with that of social interaction. This is clearly expressed by the image of the prison artfully used by Naipaul in the final part of the novel. After Salim's smuggling business has been discovered, the unpolitical man who lived for the here and now, the detached observer of social life finds himself imprisoned with other victims of the regime. He still considers himself a man apart. He is not tortured or beaten up, as happens to the other prisoners, but now he experiences a double separatedness: from the prisoners and from the people outside: "Every image that I had of that world outside was poisoned for me by what was going around me!" (279). Salim still clings to the ethics of survival and hopes he will be ransomed, but for the first time he cannot look at the external reality with indifference. He is the victim of his aloofness, because he came to Africa knowing nothing, despite the public concern expressed in the papers, about the political changes that had dramatically worsened the conditions of life in his town.

This idea of continuous political and existential metamorphosis is conveniently expressed in the novel by the image of fluidity. People, in fact, face endless political change ("Nothing stands still. Everything changes" 114), live in the flow of time in which positive experience is a mere interval, and are drawn away by events outside their control. The imagery of fluidity alludes both to (Yvette's) existential instability: "My life is still fluid" (197), and to the macroevents of politics: "But men had lost or rejected the idea of an overseeing authority, and everything was again as fluid as it had been at the beginning" (217); "[. . .] in the town, where all was arbitrary [. . .] all our lives were fluid" (198). To Salim, at first Ferdinand looks like a "solid person" (53), that is, both an integrated by-product of the Big Man's new political line and educational system, and the natural outcome of tribal Africa obviously at home in his native context. But ancestral tradition and radical innovation do not coalesce in Ferdinand's personality, which is slowly deconstructed until it too becomes shapeless: "His personality had become fluid"

(53). The semantics of fluidity are also used by Salim to illustrate the great historical events concerning his people: "One tide of history" has brought them to Africa, "another tide of history was coming" (25-26) to wash them away.

A key image artfully planted throughout the novel are the water hyacinths. They represent something peace-inspiring, outside time, untouched by the brutality of history. Salim's occasional desire for forgetfulness and quietness is embodied by the "white hyacinths," which soothe him after the evening spent at Raymond's. Water hyacinths emanate suggestions of nostalgic happiness; they may be "lilac on bright green" (164) and speak of something over, an idealized perfection which is now remote. But they especially represent a nameless hope, an inexpressible idea of beauty, righteousness, and purified humanity, which still must find the proper lexis to be transferred into experience Accordingly, the hyacinths are unknown to the local people to whom they are a new enemy: there is no word for them in the language; they are just called "the new thing in the river" (51). The river (the flow of history) takes away the bush from the heart of the continent, but some clumps of water hyacinths are the fruit of the river alone on which they are a recent appearance, just as, for many Africans, the awareness of being part of history and the necessity of governing its course is equally recent. And, in the final page of the novel, the hyacinths represent something beautiful, still unknown and untried: a *promesse du bonheur* pathetically weak and offended by man's existential and political madness:

> They were in flight from the river banks. They jammed and jostled against the sides of the steamer and the barge, and many were swamped. Water hyacinths pushed up in the narrow space between the steamer and the barge. We went on. Darkness fell. (286-87)

In the novel's ending, centred on the battle on the river, people in flight from the river banks try to take over the steamer on which Salim too is fleeing.[2] The episode takes place in darkness and conveys the connotative meaning that history is an absurd battle fought by ignorant armies clashing at night, all driven by the same stream, the flow of chance towards nothing but mere biological survival and meaningless wandering. The steamer's searchlights show thousands of insects flying in the white light, which will soon be filled with moths. The final iconic message of the text groups a sign of obscure life in the dark (moths), a sign of parasitical life in the dirt (insects), and a chromatic sign of economic power linked to the colonial past (white). For the time being, no more developed forms of existence seem to be possible in Africa.

To conclude, the vision of life and history provided by the novel is one of continuous metamorphosis and flow. Personal experience is not a continuum characterized by the succession of logical stages, but part of the fluid in which a conflict-ridden world undergoes incessant historical changes which reduce it to a shapeless and meaningless toy in the hands of a tyrant. The existence of a town and of its inhabitants may resist the space of a breath at a bend in the river: a nook of apparent rest and quietness in the course of the stream and of history. They also are soon driven away by the flow of events.

A Bend in the River has at least two other significant lessons on history to teach. The first lesson concerns the illustration of what is known to rhetoric as the argument according to direction: one may reject politics and be a separate observer of the progressive deterioration and increasing violence going around only for some time. If unhindered, that violence will inevitably be pushed further until, bit by bit, it will reach even neutral onlookers and opportunistic bystanders who indulge the illusion of being untouched by what is apparently beyond their sphere of interest.

The second lesson imparted by this postcolonial *Heart of Darkness* is that, in modern Africa, too many voices and contradictions commingle and clash to be harmonized in the span of a few generations. Although Naipaul's view is unquestionably pessimistic, he seems to imply that only through the defeat of anti-teleology, the honest historical systematization of the past, the endorsement of public accountability, and the slow downgrading of ignorance, selfishness and corruption, will Africa become a contintent in which to live, and not just an ideal place of the mind to which to turn in a nostalgic mood while wandering elsewhere.

Notes

1. Quotations from *A Bend in the River* (first published by André Deutsch in 1979) are from the 1980 Penguin edition.
2. Significantly, the final chapter of Naipaul's *North of South: An African Journey* is entitled "Into the Void" and its last phrase reads: "I fled" (349). Permanent research in darkness is, incidentally, the role Naipaul ascribes to himself in his early works of fiction: "Fiction, working its mysteries, by indirections finding directions out, had led me to my subject" (Naipaul 2000: 38).

Works Cited

Foucault, Michel. *The History of Sexuality, volume 2: The Use of Pleasure.* New York: Random House, 1986.

Gorra, Michael. *After Empire: Scott, Naipaul, Rushdie.* Chicago: Chicago UP, 1997.

Naipaul, V.S. *North of South: An African Journey.* 1978. Harmondsworth: Penguin, 1980.

——. *Reading and Writing: A Personal Account.* New York: New York Review of Books, 2000.

——. *A Bend in the River.* Harmondsworth: Penguin, 1980.

4

V.S. Naipaul's Quest for a Voice of his Own: *The Enigma of Arrival* and *Half a Life*

FLORENCE D'SOUZA

Vidiadhar Surajprasad Naipaul was born in Trinidad in 1932. He came to England on a scholarship in 1950, at the age of eighteen. He spent four years at University College, Oxford, and began to write in London in 1954, while working in the Overseas Caribbean Service of the BBC. He has followed no other profession than that of writer ever since. At the time when he obtained the Nobel Prize for Literature in December 2001, he had published twenty-six books in all: thirteen works of fiction, and thirteen works of non-fiction which include several travel accounts and three essays on India.[1]

Literary critics have reacted to Naipaul's writings in a wide variety of manners. For example, the West Indian Marxist critic Selwyn R. Cudjoe accuses Naipaul of writing "fiction of a dubious order" which "degenerates into banality" and "absurdity." Cudjoe finds that Naipaul's work "moves toward an increasing identification with the dominant imperialist ideology and racist preoccupation of the time."[2] American critics tend to be more circumspect. Paul Theroux, despite his subsequent personal estrangement from Naipaul, pays homage to the "uniqueness of his vision," and to his formal innovativeness:[3]

> Naipaul's concerns, as we have seen, remain constant: creation, fantasy and myth, homelessness, dependency,

> marriage, travel, the past. His choice of words matches his concerns [...]. Yet constant in these concerns, each of Naipaul's books has a different shape and texture [...].

While touching on the controversial aspects of Naipaul's writing, Bruce King underlines the ambivalence of the views of this "former colonial who has become a homeless cosmopolitan":[4]

> His views often have the effect of paradox and surprise, forcing a re-examination of received opinions. He objects that describing him as a West Indian writer is patronizing and limiting. A severe critic of India and the shortcomings of newly independent nations, he is also a nationalist who feels humiliated by the weakness and exploitation of the colonized; he blames European imperialism for the problems it left its former colonies, while praising it for bringing peace and modern thought to areas of the world that remained medieval and debilitated by continual local wars. There is a moral honesty in his work, a refusal to sentimentalize England or the former colonies [...].

As for Indian critics, they seem to be preoccupied with the ideological commitments and the geographical moorings of Naipaul's works. Suman Gupta notes Naipaul's "basically conservative and increasingly anti-revolutionary understanding of human spirituality and society," qualifying him as a "cultural essentialist" who achieves "aesthetically pleasing" results based on a conviction of the existence of "human truths, authentic features and universal evaluative criteria."[5] Meenakshi Mukherjee regrets Naipaul's "inexact and vague" portrayal of Indian and African realities in *Half a Life*, while wondering at these locations being "relegated to haziness."[6]

I would like to argue here that despite the rather contradictory and often negative reactions by critics to Naipaul's writing, he has definitely developed a distinct authorial voice of his own, coming as he does from a family of Eastern Uttar Pradesh Brahmins who left India for Trinidad around the 1870s, as *girmitiyas* or indentured labourers, to work in the British

Caribbean sugarcane plantations.[7] I will base my argument on two of Naipaul's later novels: *The Enigma of Arrival* (1987) and *Half a Life* (2001)[8] try to trace the author's attempts to forge a voice of his own. I will compare the generic composition of these two texts, each of which Naipaul has expressly described as a novel on their respective covers. For *The Enigma of Arrival*, Naipaul adds: "a novel in 5 sections," and for *Half a Life* he has chosen to put the following clarification on the first page: "This book is an invention. It is not exact about the countries, periods or situations it appears to describe." In his reception speech to the Nobel Committee and the Swedish Academy in December 2001, Naipaul made the following remarks about his approach to literary genres:[9]

> Both fiction and the travel-book form have given me my way of looking; and you will understand why for me all literary forms are equally valuable. It came to me, for instance, when I set out to write my third book about India—twenty-six years after the first—that what was most important about a travel book were the people the writer travelled among. The people had to define themselves. A simple enough idea, but it required a new kind of book; it called for a new way of travelling. And it was the very method I used later when I went, for the second time, into the Muslim world.

It is this eclectic, experimental play with various literary forms that enables Naipaul to express his own, unique "way of looking," which differs from book to book. Here, I will try to analyse various structural elements in the generic composition of *The Enigma of Arrival* and *Half a Life* in order to illustrate his evolving, tailor-made method of literary creation.

It is immediately striking that in both novels there is a strong autobiographical element. The trajectory of the first-person narrator in *The Enigma of Arrival* closely resembles that of V.S. Naipaul himself, with early years passed in a tropical island, literary studies in England and the ups and downs of launching a writing career. In fact, there is a frequent tantalising shift between a distanced, objective looking-back on events by the narrator and a relentless tracking of the genesis of the very text itself by the author throughout the novel. For example (*EoA* 309):[10]

> My theme, the narrative to carry it, my characters—for some years I felt they were sitting on my shoulder, waiting to declare themselves and to possess me. But it was only out of this new awareness of death that I began at last to write. Death was the motif; it had perhaps been the motif all along. Death and the way of handling it—that was the motif of the story of Jack.

This is further corroborated by the incorporation of travel accounts of journeys by the narrator. The second of the five sections, entitled "The Journey," reports the narrator's voyage from Trinidad to London in 1950, his two return trips to Trinidad in 1956 and 1960, and his arrival in Wiltshire in 1970, and terminates more than ten years later with his receipt of a letter from Angela, whom he had met in London on his first arrival in England, thirty years earlier. The last section of the book, entitled "The Ceremony of Farewell," recounts another journey to Trinidad by the narrator at the end of 1984 to attend the cremation rites of his dead sister Sati. In about the middle of the second section, "The Journey," the narrator traces the gradual fusion between Naipaul the writer and the narrator-protagonist of *The Enigma of Arrival* (*EoA* 135):

> The separation of man from writer which had begun on the long aeroplane flight from Trinidad to New York became complete. Man and writer both dwindled—the preparations of years seeming to end in futility in a few weeks. And then, but only very slowly, man and writer came together again. It was nearly five years—a year after Oxford was over for me, and long after Angela and Earls Court passed out of my ken—before I could shed the fantasies given me by my abstract education. Nearly five years before vision

> was granted me, quite suddenly one day when I was desperate for such an illumination, of what my material as a writer might be.

Similarly, *Half a Life* contains deliberately transposed versions of three fundamental aspects of Naipaul's own life and œuvre.[11] These are encapsulated in each of the three sections of the novel: a father who by his choices and attitudes greatly influences his son's life in the first part set in India; the challenges of launching into a life of writing in the second part set in London; and finally, the ambivalences of "half and half" people who have lived under a colonial regime, in the third part set in Portuguese Africa. This autobiographical aspect is underlined by the frequent use of letters in the text, which highlights the personal exchanges between the narrator and the other characters. There are two, brief, almost identically worded letters from the writer Somerset Maugham, one to Chandran Senior in India and one to Willie Chandran in London, in response to their requests to assist Willie in England. The brevity of these responses puts all possibility of assistance firmly out of the question (*HaL* 49, 58). Willie meets with similar insensitivity in a letter from a well-known London journalist who had earlier written an article on Willie's sadhu father, after a trip to India (*HaL* 56). These letters underline the communication gap between the former colonizers and the ex-colonized people. Three other letters concern Willie's sister Sarojini. The first, from the elder Chandran, is about his having arranged for Sarojini to marry an elderly German photographer; then a letter from Sarojini from Germany announces her involvement in a film on Cuba together with her intention of visiting Willie in London; and, finally, a letter from Willie to Sarojini in Charlottenburg, written from the military hospital in a town in Portuguese Africa prepares for Willie's departure for Germany after his eighteen years in Portuguese Africa. These three letters show the closeness of the brother-sister bond in Indian families despite geographical separation and differing world-views (*HaL* 112-13, 116, 136). They also mark key turning-points in the unfolding of the novel's events.

The only other letter is from the Portuguese-African woman Ana, whom Willie Chandran marries in a move to escape from his dead-end situation in London. Her letter is in reaction to a review in the *Daily Mail* of Willie's first published book and begins an acquaintance that changes the direction of Willie's life (*HaL* 124). It points to similarities in the situations and reactions of people of the "half and half" zones across all human societies, since Ana had felt a kind of moral kinship with the author of the book reviewed and this had prompted her to write him.

In *Half a Life* Naipaul transposes many autobiographical elements and uses letters between the characters to trace personal relationships over distance, although on the whole this is a much more traditional novel, with a series of events that befall clear-cut characters who seem to belong more to the realm of the imagination than do the characters in *The Enigma of Arrival*, whose role is almost external to the main issues dealt with and whose only reason for appearing in the text seems to be as the narrator's personal encounters and acquaintances.

Another angle of Naipaul's generic experimentation can be observed in his use of intertextual references. In *The Enigma of Arrival*, in the process of the protagonist-narrator's evolution and confirmation as a professional writer, a series of literary models are alluded to. Whether for their manner of evoking London, or their ambition and personality in their role as writers, or the specific characteristics of certain literary texts, or the initial reaction they provoke in the narrator, a large number of works and writers stud the text for their exemplary value. Thus we come across Dickens' old-fashioned and simple evocation of London that gives free rein to the reader's fantasy (*EoA* 123) and Somerset Maugham's elegant aloofness and unsurprised knowingness, while J.R. Ackerley, Evelyn Waugh and Aldous Huxley simultaneously inspire and frustrate the narrator (*EoA* 103, 122, 124-25). The text also presents three early literary creations of the narrator-protagonist, based on personal experiences of his ship's journey from Trinidad to Southampton and his first discoveries in London. These imaginary writings are woven into the text as part of the narrator's travel journal, marking his attempts at 'metropolitan' writing before he could decide upon his material. These exploratory works bear the titles "Gala Night," "Life in London," and "Angela" (*EoA* 112, 129, 137, 143), but they only constitute tentative experiments to be left behind as the narrator moves on to determine his own, personal literary domain.

This brings us to the narrator's aesthetic manifesto, which appears in an undidactic, hit-and-miss manner at three points in the text. It can be understood as a Nietzschean, Dionysian transmutation of the fatality of decay and inevitable death, with a refusal of the hyper-rationalized Apollonian or Brahmanical order that is cut and dried from the outset. Instead, the narrator espouses a lucid resistance through artistic creation that tries to interpret and make sense of life and reality in an outburst of life-affirming activity that has to be constantly renewed.[12] Naipaul's narrator's version of the Nietzschean vision is presented as entering into writing "as I might enter a walled garden or enclosure," as a means of strengthening himself and quelling anxiety (*EoA* 154). In a parallel between the landlord of the Manor House, on whose grounds he rents a cottage, and himself, the narrator records delight in decay, perceived as flux and constant change (*EoA* 195):

> It would have been like my own wish, coming to the cottage in his grounds, not to interfere, to take things as I found them; and then my later wish, out of my own delight in the place, not to see decay, not to be saddened by that too ready idea of decay, to see instead flux, constant change; and the feeling which I grew to cherish, that in the very dereliction of the grounds I had come upon them at their peak, that the order created by sixteen gardeners would have been too much, would have made for strain and anxiety, that the true beauty of the place lay in accidental, unintended things [...].

It is thus a paradoxical act of unaffirmative self-affirmation that does not seek to impose an external, rational order on things, but rather to transmute the perception of the existing state of things into something with a personal sense, that Naipaul and his narrator find their self-statement. He is aware of the danger and risk of morbidity and inertia that this entails, as embodied by his passive landlord (*EoA* 254):

> Perhaps he had stalled in what might be considered a state of perfection. But that perfection—that absence of restlessness and creative abrasion, that view from his back windows of a complete, untouched, untroubled world—had turned to morbidity, accidia, a death of the soul.

On the contrary, the narrator's own encounter with death (when his sister dies in Trinidad) makes him aware of the need to remake the world for himself, which he proceeds to do in the act of writing (*EoA* 318):

> But we remade the world for ourselves; every generation does that, as we found when we came together for the death of this sister and felt the need to honour and remember. It forced us to look on death. It forced me to face the death I had been contemplating at night, in my sleep; it fitted a real grief where melancholy had created a vacancy, as if to prepare me for the moment. It showed me life and man as the mystery, the true religion of men, the grief and the glory. And that was when, faced with a real death, and with this new wonder about men, I laid aside my drafts and hesitations and began to write very fast about Jack and his garden.

Another intertextual thread with Nietzschean overtones in *The Enigma of Arrival* revolves around a painting done in Paris in the winter of 1911-1912, by the Italian Giorgio de Chirico (1888-1978), from which the book draws its title. From 1909-1919, de Chirico developed his own style of "metaphysical painting" with distinct literary inspiration (in particular under the influence of Nietzsche's writings), in an attempt to interpret the enigmas of life and the universe. De Chirico's paintings use the potential polyvalence of concrete objects (like a funeral edifice, a chequered floor surface, a blank wall, the sail and mast of a ship) to suggest mystery and strangeness in a metaphorical evocation of the cycle of life. They evoke themes like the sea, travel, the melancholy of departure, danger, adventure and the unknown.[13] De Chirico's painting gives rise to three textual improvisations in Naipaul's text. In the first version (*EoA* 92), Naipaul's narrator imagines a story "set in classical times, in the Mediterranean" where the protagonist, on arriving at the port, experiences "silence and desolation." On escaping from the crowded city back to the quayside of arrival, he discovers the antique ship has gone, marking a kind of dead end. In the second version (*EoA* 156-157), the precise geographical setting gives way to a greater focus on the character's "spasm of fear" and reluctance to disembark in an alien, unknown land. It ends again with an erasure of the means of departure, but also establishes a parallel with Naipaul's narrator's own story, thus opening on to a more personalized interpretation. In the third version, which appears in the final section (*EoA* 309-10), the "Mediterranean fantasy" is metamorphosed into a story of "the writer's journey" (*EoA* 309), marking the magical, mysterious transmutation of a story of personal adventures and experiences into an aestheticised narrative of writing discoveries and the writer's ways of seeing, heralding a fusion of writer and man, who had been separate at the beginning of the journey. Thus, intertexts enable Naipaul to develop several aspects of this self-reflexive work, operating as loops in the elaboration of his aesthetic manifesto.

In *Half a Life*, intertextual references seem to have a more parodic, satirical intention than in *The Enigma of Arrival*. The first section, entitled "A Visit from Somerset Maugham," can be read as a satirical rewriting of R.K. Narayan's *The Guide*.[14] Several elements of Narayan's novel appear in a modified form in *Half a Life*. For example, Narayan's protagonist, the tourist guide known as Railway Raju, takes refuge in the courtyard of a temple after being released from a prison sentence for embezzlement, and makes a new career as a holy man, receiving alms and donations in exchange for his wise advice. In Naipaul's novel, the narrator's father, the elder Chandran, had taken refuge in a temple courtyard in his town to escape the persecution of the local maharaja's officials, because of a charge of corruption in his job at the maharaja's Land Tax department (*HaL* 2). Thanks to his vow of silence, he had reacquired a social status, accompanied by respect and renown. The satire becomes evident when the elder Chandran confesses that this course of action occurred to him because his own grandfather (the narrator's great-grandfather) had similarly found refuge and free subsistence in the temple courtyard of the local state's capital, when faced with starvation and unemployment in the temple of his native village (*HaL* 5). Also, the elder Chandran confesses that his new temple courtyard life amounted to "living as a mendicant on the alms of the poorest of the poor" (*HaL* 3). So, not only is blind repetition of bygone, ancestral tradition as advocated by Brahmins denounced here, but its parasitical nature is underlined. In *Half a Life*, Somerset Maugham's visit to the elder Chandran in his temple courtyard, the English author's mention of the information he obtained during the exchange in a subsequent book of travel souvenirs, suddenly transforming the renegade, elder Chandran into a very respectable person in the eyes of the local population, and the use of Indian spiritual sources for Maugham's famous novel *The Razor's Edge*, subsequently traced to the elder Chandran by foreign critics (*HaL* 3), can be seen as a parodic rewriting of the role of Marco, a European Indologist in Narayan's *The Guide*. Marco visits Malgudi to decipher stone inscriptions in the Iswara Temple (*The Guide* 56) and publishes his research in a scholarly book later, with printed acknowledgement of Raju's assistance (*The Guide* 175). The satire in Naipaul's version lies in the reaction of the local population and in the detective work by foreign critics to trace Maugham's sources on Indian spirituality.

The platonic relationship between Narayan's characters, the impresario Raju and the gifted Bharat Natyam dancer Rosie, can be seen as a likely source for the iconoclastic relationship, deliberately outside the strict Brahmanical norms for endogamous marriage, between the elder Chandran and his low-caste wife. Naipaul's satirical intentions become clear in the elder Chandran's declaration to his son that no marriage ceremony ever took place between him and his 'wife,' and that despite his vow of *brahmacharya* or sexual abstinence, two children were born of the union, namely the protagonist Willie Chandran and his sister Sarojini (*HaL* 33, 35)!

Another intertextual thread in *Half a Life* links the protagonist's life in Portuguese Africa, where he has an affair with the half-Portuguese Graça, to his childhood in India "about twenty-five years before" (*HaL* 206). It exposes the equivocal attribution of unquestionable moral integrity to all the acts of the characters in Brahmanical legends and epics. Here, the reference is to King Dasaratha, father of Lord Rama of the epic Ramayana. Dasaratha is known to have had three wives. In Willie Chandran's childhood memory, a local merchant had visited his sage father in his ashram (a sacred abode, that had followed upon the sojourn in the temple courtyard) to seek advice and comfort, since according to him he was like King Dasaratha inasmuch as he had two wives. However, far from condoning this imitation of King Dasaratha, the elder Chandran had scolded the merchant on two accounts—first, for his presumption in comparing himself to gods and second, for his "squalid bazaar lusts" and "shamelessness!" (*HaL* 206-07) This reaction of the elder Chandran had upheld the honour of the community and 'added' to his reputation! The glaring contradiction between the impulse to imitate the epic's paternal figure and the indictment it met with is further heightened by Willie Chandran's own subsequent distancing from his father's Brahmanical stand, since twenty-five years later, in his own, illicit relationship with Graça, Willie feels "gratitude" for Graça's love, faces his own wife Ana "without shame" and deals with

Graça's husband with genuine "friendship!" (*HaL* 207) A long way indeed from the example and the Brahminical interpretation of the age-old Ramayana!

Yet another ironical intertext is linked to Willie Chandran's reference to both the text and the film of Hemingway's short story "The Killers" and to the film version of "The Childhood of Maxim Gorky," from which, on his lawyer friend Roger's advice, he draws inspiration for his first attempts at short-story writing (*HaL* 83, 84, 88). He makes the paradoxical discovery that borrowed settings, borrowed stories and imagined characters "far outside himself" were in fact easier to handle when writing and enabled him "to be truer to his feelings" than "direct tales from his own life or the life around him" (*HaL* 86). He is however seized by compunctions and self-doubt about his fictional "game" when about to meet Ana, his first reader-enthusiast (*HaL* 125-26):

> But if she came and questioned him too closely about his book he might find himself giving the game away, and the woman or girl with the Portuguese-sounding name might understand that the Indian stories in which she had seen aspects of her own African life had been borrowed from old Hollywood movies and the Maxim Gorky trilogy from Russia. Willie didn't want the woman to be let down. He wanted her to stay an admirer. This line of thinking led him the other way, to worrying about himself. He began to worry that the woman might not find him good enough for the book he had written, not attractive enough or with presence enough.

Apart from the use of intertexts with self-reflexive, aesthetic connotations or outright satirical intentions, Naipaul uses a musical type of structural form in both *The Enigma of Arrival* and *Half a Life*: "theme and variations." It involves the recurrence with varied developments of particular themes or motifs at different points of these two texts.

One such theme that appears several times in *The Enigma of Arrival* is the theme of the garden, always linked to the idea of decay, be it the workman Jack's cottage garden or the Manor House Garden or the narrator's memories of gardens in Trinidad. Jack's cottage garden, remarked for its well-tended hedge, beds, plots and vegetable allotment, is compared to "a medieval village in miniature" (*EoA* 22), which has taught the narrator about the seasons and brought fulfilment and satisfaction to Jack (*EoA* 32-33). Then, as Jack becomes ill, his garden becomes "wild" leaving "only a ruin," to end up "flattened" and "grassed over" (*EoA* 43, 47, 58), marking the inevitable changes wrought by the passing of time. Likewise, the Manor House grounds, despite their grandeur, including an orchard, a walled vegetable garden, lawns, a drive and paths, and pear-trees on the squash-court wall, bear the signs of decay in the reduction in the number of gardeners employed to tend them- from a force of sixteen regular gardeners, the grounds came to be tended by the single-handed Pitton and even he had to go, leaving their care in the hands of occasional contract workers (*EoA* 60). The Manor House grounds overlooking the river, the water meadows and the bare downs beyond, embody perfection as painted by Constable on the one hand, and debilitating corruption on the other (*EoA* 185-86):

> But perfection such as my landlord looked out on contained its own corruption. Perfection like that could too easily be taken for granted. There was nothing in that view (of ivy and forest debris and choked water meadow) which would irritate or encourage doubt; there was nothing in that view which would encourage action in a man already spiritually weakened by personal flaws, disappointments and, above all, his knowledge of his own great security. The view—so complete, so simple—seemed to say or could appear to say: "This is the world. Why worry? Why interfere?"

This link with decay in the Manor House grounds is associated with such telling symbols as ivy (*EoA* 196-197), rooks, known to augur death or money (*EoA* 266, 276, 281), and the snapping of venerable aspen trees, leaving dead stumps that are gradually overrun by weeds (*EoA* 162, 237, 249, 254, 300). The final touch to this theme with variations on gardens and decay is achieved through a contrast with the "unskilled," "debased" town occupation associated with gardening in Trinidad, where colonial-type agricultural exploitation of sugar-cane, cocoa and later vegetable plots in former swamps had eradicated the "childhood delight in making things grow," leaving, in the place of childlike magic, only adult "servitude and ugliness" (*EoA* 203-05, 215-16). This theme is therefore a vehicle for evocations of differing world-views, attitudes to nature and perceptions of the passage of time.

Another theme that occurs several times in *The Enigma of Arrival* is the narrator's dream of an explosion in his head, staging various versions of his own death. It enables the narrator to suggest the exhaustion, grief, great tiredness and personal crisis he went through along his way to becoming a writer (*EoA* 93, 96-97, 156, 179). This upsetting dream is later replaced by "a great melancholy" that poisons the narrator's life like a penetrating "gloom" (*EoA* 309), until an external crisis (the death of his sister in Trinidad) triggers a revelation in him that inspired him to write *The Enigma of Arrival.* This dream of the exploding head therefore serves as a note of discord that leads on to a subsequent harmonious resolution in the unfolding of the text.

Similarly in *Half a Life,* though on a less ambitious scale than in *The Enigma of Arrival,* at least two motifs can be observed in varied renderings. One such theme is the loss and reconstruction of identity. Soon after his arrival in London, Willie Chandran finds that he has "to re-learn everything that he knew" in order to blend in with his new environment—this includes how to greet people, how to close doors, and how to ask for things (*HaL* 59). While presenting himself to all his new acquaintances, Willie enjoys the "dizzying" possibilities of playing with words to "re-make himself and his past and his ancestry" (*HaL* 60). He renders all these aspects of himself a little grander than in reality through his choice of terms to describe them. The theme of the loss of identity is linked to the idea of cultural and social difference, causing an oscillation between acceptance and rejection. From a barrier of exclusion or a weapon of defence, against awkward rules or cruelties, Willie Chandran overcomes this "feeling of distance" from those around him in the "unquestioning" approach of Ana, who from her own "half-and-half position" gives him "this new feeling of being accepted" completely (*HaL* 125-26), making possible a feeling of wholeness in him for the first time, "as a man and being in his own eyes complete." On the ship journey between Southampton and Portuguese Africa with Ana, Willie is seized with a "worry about the loss of language"—since in Portuguese Africa neither his home language nor English is spoken (*HaL* 132-33). A minor crisis takes the form of the momentary loss of Willie's passport in Ana's estate home. It is resolved when under a threat of a visit from the fetish man, the lost passport suddenly resurfaces in the drawers of the bureau (*HaL* 158-59). The final appearance of this theme in the novel takes on a tragic tone when, in the face of a civil war and the takeover of the country by a new regime, Graça is forced to accept the departure of her children for Portugal. She finds it ridiculous that in Portugal they will have to "prepare papers to say who they are" (*HaL* 226). She feels more secure in her paperless identity in the place where her grandfather and ancestors are buried (*HaL* 226). Her position appears quite tragic when the narrator refers to the look in her eyes as "suffering" and qualifies her as "a deranged person." She could be perceived as an embodiment of the possibility of total alienation and irremediable unbelonging that threatens all persons in any kind of "half and half position."

Another very striking motif appears twice in *Half a Life*: it is the image of a spitting cobra. The first time it occurs, it is linked to the ruins of an abandoned estate house known as the "German

Castle" because it was built by a German in the 1920s or 1930s. It is the place where Willie and Graça choose to consummate their physical attraction to each other. The place is pervaded by "a strange smell of fish" which turns out to be caused by spitting cobras inside the castle. Thus despite Willie's discovery of an unknown "depth of satisfaction" in his lovemaking with Graça, the disturbing presence of unseen, spitting cobras, perceived only through the smell they emit, but which could blind someone from a distance of many feet, throws an atmosphere of unpleasantness and decay on the whole episode (*HaL* 204-05). The same motif of the spitting cobra with its disturbing quality appears again in the house of Ana's half-brother. The fact that he lives in the African shanty settlement known as "the city of cane" (*HaL* 213), on the edge of the town proper, sets the tone. This dark-skinned man with light eyes, given to aggressive showing off, keeps, as a personal treasure, a living, spitting cobra imprisoned in a green-tinted bottle, and takes pleasure in tormenting and teasing it, resulting in the snake's lashing about and exuding "some kind of mucus" (*HaL* 215-16) from its mouth. The shocking, disgusting effect created by the imprisoned snake is quite spectacular, especially since it appears suddenly without warning in the text. It can be understood to portray a whole host of things - potential evil, oppression, repressed or frustrated sexuality, danger, thwarted individuality, a frenetic search for statement. The text refrains from giving this motif any specific signification, deliberately leaving it open to the reader's interpretation. Its unsettling impact is however undeniable.

In both these novels, therefore, certain motifs are deliberately incorporated several times over, with a different development at each appearance, creating an impression of structural coherence in a textual imitation of musical composition. Through all these generic and aesthetic experiments, which show a creative disrespect and liberty with regard to established norms and forms, Naipaul's message seems to be that whatever the individual's place in social and political systems might be, life's goal and orientation have constantly to be reinvented and rediscovered. He leaves the reader with the overall feeling that his voice as a writer is the unique, vital rampart of his identity. His two novels *The Enigma of Arrival* and *Half a Life* can be seen as literary illustrations of his open-ended, continually improvised exploration of this inimitable, innermost fibre of himself.

Notes

1. See Works Cited.
2. Selwyn R. Cudjoe, *V.S. Naipaul—a Materialist Reading* (Amherst: U of Massachusetts P, 1988) 15.
3. Paul Theroux, *V.S. Naipaul—an Introduction to his Work* (London: André Deutsch, 1972) 130-31; 135.
4. Bruce King, *V.S. Naipaul* (London: Macmillan, 1993) 2.
5. Suman Gupta, *V.S. Naipaul* (Plymouth: Northcote House, 1999) 59, 91, 98.
6. Meenakshi Mukherjee, "A House for Mr. Naipaul," *Frontline* 18.22 (2001).
7. V.S. Naipaul, "Two Worlds," Nobel Lecture, 7 Dec. 2001: "We made no inquiries about India or about the families people had left behind. When our ways of thinking had changed and we wished to know, it was too late. I know nothing of the people on my father's side; I know only that some of them came from Nepal. Two years ago a kind Nepalese who liked my name sent me a copy of some pages from an 1872 gazetteer-like British work about India, *Hindu castes and Tribes as represented in Benares*; the pages listed - among a multitude of names - those groups of Nepalese in the holy city of Banaras who carried the name Naipal. That is all that I have."
8. V.S. Naipaul, *The Enigma of Arrival* (Harmondsworth: Penguin, 1987): the quotations from this text will be accompanied by the abbreviation *EoA* and the corresponding page number; V.S. Naipaul, *Half a Life* (London: Picador, 2001): the quotations from this text will be accompanied by the abbreviation *HaL* and the corresponding page number.
9. V.S. Naipaul, "Two Worlds," Nobel Lecture, 7 Dec. 2001.
10. See Florence Labaune-Demeule, "V.S. Naipaul's Reconciliation with Himself: the Ultimate *Enigma of Arrival*," *Commonwealth* 23.1

(Autumn 2000): 59-70, where she traces the oscillations between the voice of the narrator-protagonist and the voice of the author-man, culminating in a fusion between fiction and reality in the text.

11. See article by Amit Chaudhuri, "Learning how to write," *Times Literary Supplement* 21 Sept. 2001: 22-23.
12. See Nietzsche, *La Naissance de la Tragédie* (1872; Paris: Christian Bourgois, 1991) 12, 24. See also Gilles Deleuze, *Nietzsche et la philosophie* (Paris: Presses Universitaires de France, 1962) 223-26.
13. See Paolo Baldacci, *Chirico - la métaphysique, 1888-1919* (Paris: Flammarion, 1997) 61-66, 83, 118-20. See also Florence Labaune-Demeule, "De Chirico revisited: The enigma of creation in V.S. Naipaul's *The Enigma of Arrival*," *Commonwealth* 22.2 (Spring 2000): 107-18: her study of the links between De Chirico's painting and Naipaul's text traces the transcending of experience and memory through an effort of mental interiorization and the imagination, as a means to self-knowledge, endowing experience with a new coherence and "a new harmonious pattern." This innovating, aestheticising process remains an unexplainable mystery in both De Chirico's and Naipaul's works, according to the author of the article.
14. R.K. Narayan, *The Guide* (1958; Harmondsworth: Penguin, 1988).

Works Cited

Baldacci, Paolo. *Chirico - la métaphysique 1888-1919*. Paris: Flammarion, 1997.

Chaudhuri, Amit. "Learning how to Write." *Times Literary Supplement* 21 Sept. 2001: 22-23.

Cudjoe, Selwyn R. *V.S. Naipaul—a Materialist Reading*. Amherst: U of Massachusetts P, 1988.

Damase, Jacques, ed. *De Chirico par De Chirico*. Paris: Jacques Damase, 1978.

Deleuze, Gilles. *Nietzsche et la philosophie*. Paris: Presses Universitaires de France, 1962.

Gupta, Suman. *V.S. Naipaul*. Plymouth: Northcote House, 1999.

King, Bruce. *V.S. Naipaul*. London: Macmillan, 1993.

Labaune-Demeule, Florence. "De Chirico Revisited: The Enigma of Creation in V.S. Naipaul's *The Enigma of Arrival*." *Commonwealth* 22.2 (Spring 2000): 107-18.

——. "V.S. Naipaul's Reconciliation with Himself: The Ultimate *Enigma of Arrival*." *Commonwealth* 23.1 (Autumn 2000): 59-70.

Mukherjee, Meenakshi. "A House for Mr. Naipaul." *Frontline* 18.22 (2001). <http://www.hinduonnet.com/fline/fl1822/18220520.htm>.

Naipaul, V.S. *The Mystic Masseur*. London: André Deutsch, 1957.

——. *The Suffrage of Elvira*. London: André Deutsch, 1958.

——. *Miguel Street*. London: André Deutsch; New York: Vanguard, 1959.

——. *A House for Mr Biswas*. London: André Deutsch; New York: McGraw-Hill, 1961.

——. *The Middle Passage*. London: André Deutsch; New York: Macmillan, 1962.

——. *Mr Stone and the Knights Companion*. London: André Deutsch; New York: Macmillan, 1963.

——. *An Area of Darkness*. London: André Deutsch, 1964.

——. *The Mimic Men*. London: André Deutsch; New York: Macmillan, 1967.

——. *A Flag on the Island*. London: André Deutsch; New York: Macmillan, 1967.

——. *The Loss of El Dorado*. London: André Deutsch, 1969.

——. *In a Free State*. London: André Deutsch; New York: Knopf, 1971.

——. *The Overcrowded Barracoon*. London: André Deutsch, 1972.

——. *Guerrillas*. London: André Deutsch; New York; Knopf, 1975.

——. *India: A Wounded Civilization*. London: André Deutsch; New York: Knopf, 1977.

——. *A Bend in the River*. London: André Deutsch; New York: Knopf, 1979.

——. *The Return of Eva Peron* with *The Killings in Trinidad*. London: André Deutsch; New York: Knopf, 1980.

——. *Among the Believers: An Islamic Journey*. London: André Deutsch; New York: Knopf, 1981.

——. *Finding the Centre: Two Narratives*. London: André Deutsch; New York: Knopf, 1984.

——. *The Enigma of Arrival*. London: Viking, 1987.

——. *A Turn in the South*. London: André Deutsch; New York: Knopf, 1989.

——. *India: A Million Mutinies Now*. London: André Deutsch; New York: Viking, 1990.

——. *A Way in the World*. London: Heinemann; New York: Knopf, 1994.

——. *Beyond Belief: Islamic Excursions among the Converted Peoples*. London: Little, Brown & Co., 1998.

——. *Between Father & Son: Family Letters*. London: Little, Brown & Co., 1999; New York: Vintage Books, 2001.

——. *Reading & Writing: A Personal Account.* New York: New York Review of Books Inc., 2000.

——. *Half a Life.* London: Picador, 2001.

——. "Two Worlds." Nobel Lecture, 7 Dec. 2001. <http://www.nobel.se/literature/laureates/2001/naipaul-lecture-e.html, n.p.>

Narayan, R.K. *The Guide.* 1958. Harmondsworth: Penguin, 1988.

Nietzsche, Frédéric. *La Naissance de la Tragédie* [The Birth of Tragedy]. 1872. Paris: Christian Bourgois, 1991.

Rushdie, Salman. "V.S. Naipaul." *Imaginary Homelands—Essays & Criticism 1981-1991.* London: Granta Books, 1991. 148-51.

Theroux, Paul. *V.S. Naipaul—An Introduction to his Work.* London: André Deutsch, 1972.

Theroux, Paul. *Sir Vidia's Shadow—a Friendship across Five Continents.* New York: Houghton Mifflin, 2000.

5

"I AM THE SUM OF MY BOOKS": THE TRAILS, TRIALS, AND TRIBULATIONS OF V.S. NAIPAUL

HARALD LEUSMANN

Towards the end of his Nobel Lecture "Two Worlds" on December 7, 2001 in Stockholm, V.S. Naipaul emphasized how much joy he has experienced during his life as a writer: "I am glad to have done what I have done, glad creatively to have pushed myself as far as I could go [...]. But the greatest miracle for me was getting started. I feel—and the anxiety is still vivid to me—that I might easily have failed before I began" ("Two Worlds" 9-10). Willie Somerset Chandran, the protagonist of Naipaul's most recently published novel *Half a Life*, is not allowed to experience this miracle. Willie fails right at the beginning, in London in the 1950s, where he, inexperienced and an immigrant as Naipaul was himself, roams the streets in rain or fog until, out of the blue, he stumbles across a freelancing job with the BBC, as, what coincidence, Naipaul also did. Unlike Naipaul, however, Willie is not very decisive; nor does he have the will to use his talent to pursue the presumptuous as well as vague wish to become a writer.

Although there are a few stories that Willie is able to pen, it is no more than a trickle running dry after an initial outburst of creativity. He is unable to continue writing because of an inability to push himself past a presumed emptiness that occurs when it seems that one does not have a theme to write about. The short stories in the only collection he publishes in London mix cheap Hollywood movie plots with remembrances of his childhood in rural India. They are sad farces circling around aspects of feigned identities: "The stories seemed to be just waiting for him; he was surprised he hadn't seen them before; and he wrote fast for three or four weeks. The writing then began to lead him to difficult things, things he couldn't face, and he stopped" (*Half a Life* 96). Years later, on an estate in the Portuguese colony of Mozambique, Willie's wife Ana will tell him that she was fascinated with the motif of the fabricated life-story in his short stories because she came to recognize her own life in them: "That was just before I met you. I think you will see now why your stories spoke to me. All the bluff, the make-believe, with the real unhappiness. It was uncanny. It was why I wrote" (*Half a Life* 146).

In Stockholm, Naipaul further explained that his identity as a writer as well as a human being is inextricably linked to the books he has written throughout his life: "Everything of value about me is in my books [...]. I will say I am the sum of my books. Each book, intuitively sensed and, in the case of fiction, intuitively worked out, stands on what has gone before, and grows out of it [...] [A]t any stage of my literary career it could have been said that the last book contained all the others" ("Two Worlds" 1, 2). Consequently, *Half a Life* can be considered a distillate of aspects he touched upon in previous books: the sorrow of exile, the inseparable inclusion of his family history in the stories, the powerful maelstrom of postcolonial dissolvings leading to what Naipaul once termed 'half-made societies and half-made nations.' All these themes are bundled in the story of Willie Somerset Chandran, who drifts through three continents and three only half-finished sketches of existences until in the end at the age of forty-one he tells his sister Sarojini, on a snowy day in West Berlin, about his apathetic attempts and failures: "I have been hiding from myself. I have risked nothing. And now the best part of my life is over" (*Half a Life* 130).

This is a rather pessimistic view for someone who has travelled widely, because one of the consequences of travelling frequently is that one is always and constantly somewhere, namely in the company of oneself. One is inclined to say that this motto is, in different shades and evaluations, applicable to Naipaul himself. This experience is also manifest in the character of Leonard Side in *A Way in the World,* who is memorable for nothing else than his predilection for decorating living as well as dead people with flowers. At the beginning of that novel the young Naipaul leaves his home country only to experience alienation after each of his few returns. For instance, the people seem to be darker than he could remember them; he plays with his impressions as he played with his glasses: "[...] looking at a world now sharp and small and not quite real, now standard size and real but blurred" (*A Way in the World* 3). For a long time he can perceive these altering feelings as pleasant: they even remind him of times when he got a fever every time the rainy season started. It is in one of the periods of fever that he meets Leonard Side, who will die exactly as he lived: surrounded by bouquets of flowers and cloths made of satin and silk which serve to decorate the interior of coffins and to put a person's body to lie in state.

In the course of *A Way in the World* the narrator changes the tone and does not perceive the Other as a 'sick person' but takes on the position of an explorer or scientist who intends to enlighten the darkness of a life that is unfathomable to him so far. He wants to reconstruct both the individual and the collective story of people—if they are not capable of doing so by themselves. The lineage of ancestors reaches back into infinity, "to the very beginning; in our blood and bone and brain we carry the memories of thousands of beings [...]. We cannot understand all the traits we have inherited. Sometimes we can be strangers to ourselves" (*A Way in the World* 11).

The experience of inner alienation turns out to be the driving force of writing, and in the end even leads to a position of strength. It is not important to emphasize style—what counts is to have a vision and that one writes from a position of strength. Shaped by the wish to paint a whole culture and the outlines of the world within the individual and the regional, Naipaul was able to find the right tone already early in his novels and investigations.

The son of Indian immigrants to Trinidad and a member of the highest caste, a brahmin, Naipaul is not only the narrator or reporter who perceives a displeasing situation as a sensation. It is also always his own life that he puts on display, and it is a broken ethos that he as a philosopher of culture has to defend. However, his empathy concerning the people he encounters on his travels and whose lives and cultures he describes is broken. He has never shied away from voicing vehemently and inconsiderately his dislike of certain cultural expressions. In *The Middle Passage*, for instance, as soon as the ship that had taken Naipaul from England back to Trinidad on a tour of the Caribbean docked in Port of Spain, "I began to feel all my old fear of Trinidad" together with the resentment of the steel bands that "used to be regarded as a high manifestation of West Indian culture, and it was a sound I detested" (*The Middle Passage* 43). A few sentences later he describes Trinidad as "unimportant, uncreative, cynical," a country in which "[p]ower was recognized, but dignity was allowed to no one" (*The Middle Passage* 43). It is not only Trinidad, his birthplace, that he detests: it is the region as a whole that Naipaul feels compelled to criticise harshly, with the infamous utterance:

> For nothing was created in the British West Indies, no civilization as in Spanish America, no great revolution as in Haiti or the American colonies. There were only plantations, prosperity, decline, neglect: the size of the islands called for nothing else [...]. History is built around achievement and creation; and nothing was created in the West Indies (*The Middle Passage* 27, 29).

Beginning with his early satires and political arguments

about Trinidad around 1957/58 and continuing with the grief of his first, impressive book on India (*An Area of Darkness*), Naipaul remains a loner and a non-conformist thinker in all of his following attempts to understand Indian history, to document and narrate it—particularly narrating it, because in his understanding of himself he has never been anyone else but a narrator. In short stories, portraits, essays, novellas, and reports Naipaul writes about the Caribbean, Latin America, Africa, and Asia: *The Loss of El Dorado* (1969), *In a Free State* and *Guerrillas* (1975), *India: A Wounded Civilization* (1977), *A Bend in the River* (1979). The latter, set in a country which is nameless but identifiable as Zaire (the Congo) is written from the perspective of a non-African entering that particular country. It is this perspective of an outside person observing a foreign culture as an explorer which Naipaul perfects in his books explicitly dealing with Islam. In both *Among the Believers* (1981) and *Beyond Belief* (1998) Naipaul condemns Islam as catastrophic, a belief-system that, like colonialism, attempts to enslave or destroy other cultures.

Naipaul has been accused of being a Hindu nationalist who supports the clash of cultures on a literary level. His latest novel, *Half a Life,* continues the search and maintains his pitiless attitude towards the 'Third World': radical self-descriptions, in the end, are taking place in foreign places. The half a life which is made possible for the people of colonial and postcolonial countries is also granted to the novel's protagonist, Willie Somerset Chandran. It is in this character's failed fulfilment of his life that Naipaul licks his own wounds. Being the son of a man who disobeyed the caste rules and married a girl from a lower caste, Willie fails at life as well as love. He is a victim—the son of a mother and of a father who send their son away with the words:

> We've created a monster. He really hates his mother and his mother's people, and she doesn't know. But his mother's

> uncle was the firebrand of the backwards. I mustn't forget that. The boy will poison what remains of my life. I must get him far away from here (*Half a Life* 41-42).

No one in this scenario is able to react with love. Self-determination is not able to blossom fully in this climate, and spirituality regresses into self-castigation or loses itself in physical desires. Naipaul is Willie as well as his counterpart, as he does not want to play the role of the victim any more. This behaviour results in the striking display of manners comparable to those of a British conservative: contemptuous to all those who do not acknowledge values of Western civilization such as individuality, intellectuality, free choice, self-responsibility, and self-realization.

Naipaul has repeatedly emphasized that he became a writer only because of his effort of will. He has made himself the theme of many of his writings, due to a lack of subject-matter which he could have seized possession of. But right here what is revealed is the depth of a life which is searching for revelation in itself and creates characters experimenting with self-denial, finding one's self and searching for meaning. All of them, the author included, fail to reach an intellectuality in which the absence of an all-encompassing theme could prove to be the chance for a life beyond egocentrism and self-distance.

Naipaul is a traveller, a cosmopolitan with a, historically speaking, universal philosophy, a specialist when it comes to describe societal changes and intolerance, chauvinism, fanaticism and religious fundamentalism, decline, defeat, failure, and disgrace, but also the minimum hope for the remnants of a culture's pride and self-respect. To accuse him of imperial tendencies and see him as an uncritical apologist for industrial-colonial nations would be to misunderstand the agility of his observations, his transcultural point of view and his personal ethics. He collects stories that become scenic remembrances in his books, scripts of life, of a researched history and of imagination, as is manifest in the description of the landscape of Trinidad according to Naipaul's early perception as an adolescent on the island, according to historical documents from the times of European colonization, and according to his perception when living in a mansion in Wiltshire where he has finally made his home:

> In my mind's eye I created an imaginary landscape for the aboriginal peoples living—on what was to become my own ground—with ideas I couldn't enter, ideas of time, distance, the past, the natural world, human existence. A different weather seemed to attach to this vanished landscape (like the unnatural weather in an illuminated painted panorama in a museum glasscase), a different sky (*A Way in the World* 213-14).

The documentary reports *The Return of Eva Peron* (1980) and *Finding the Centre* (1984) circle around the themes of homelessness, insecurity, exile and the collision of tradition and modernity. They deal with: the aftermath of the military junta in Argentina; the 'revolution'; the Black Panthers in Trinidad; the alleged liberation movement in Guyana; Mobutism in Zaire in 1975 in the case of *The Return of Eva Peron*; and faded glory, wealth and modernity in the Ivory Coast, a documentary account written in fourteen parts over nine months in 1982/83 for *Finding the Centre*. Closely connected with these accounts is an essay on Joseph Conrad which Naipaul wrote in 1974. Although he admires Conrad as a great "stylist," "the late starter, holding out hope to those who didn't seem to be starting at all" (*The Return of Eva Peron* 207), he criticizes Conrad for not having the willingness to let a story speak for itself. Naipaul shares this opinion with H.G. Wells, who in a review of *An Outcast of the Islands* characterized the book as "wordy" and that Conrad still had to learn "the great half of his art, the art of leaving things unwritten" (*The Return of Eva Peron* 211). The "multiplicity of Conrads" which Naipaul observes remain for him "flawed" (*The Return of Eva Peron* 213), but when it comes to aestheticism in terms of not inventing countries and people anew he feels closely connected to him.

Naipaul is, on the one hand, a player of living and eloquent interactions; on the other hand, he is able to indulge in details in order to decipher all that is destructive and tyrannical, even in situations in which people believe they are safe and unrecognized behind their signs and masks, as in the case of the Ivory Coast and its capital Yamoussoukro after independence. Especially in places like this where the representation of power seems to manifest itself in the brightest colours, as a true "monumental city meant to make an African ruler immortal" (*Finding the Centre* 86), "bursting with its own powers" (*Centre* 78), one can feel the fear of the people up front; and it tastes unreal and stale. At the same time, the Ivory Coast of the early 1980s can be described as an enclave in the midst of chaos, bankruptcy, and decay on the African continent, if one compares it to the "murderous tyranny" of Guinea with the infamous "'black diet' of its condemned cells, where people were given neither food nor water and simply left to waste away" (*Centre* 81), or Ghana's anarchy after several military coups. Although Yamoussoukro, "the great enterprise" (*Centre* 86), was erected to represent traditional as well as modern times, the Ivory Coast remains in a provisional state that was supposed to guarantee high esteem and reputation among the world's nations. Consequently, the president is forced to select his successor from among the people of his tribal affiliation, a procedure intended to ensure the 'right' succession. He regards himself as a democrat and anti-tribalist though—every democratisation reaches its natural, i.e. traditional, boundaries. When he had loosened the prevailing election procedures in his country, more than eighty per cent of the previous members of parliament, several of whom had served for more than twenty years, were not re-elected. For them, that result was considered a personal disgrace, because once a man has become an 'elder' he is supposed to remain in office until he dies. In this way the democratic experiment disturbed this particular political life and coherence in the country, and was substituted again by the African concept of "reconciliation" (*Centre* 85).

This example demonstrates that Naipaul is able to identify with the host culture and uses its standards and criteria for his evaluation. He is driven by an innate curiosity to go on intellectual adventures in places which are populated by people who lead restricted lives. He follows his instincts and the curiosity of a writer, not so much that of an ethnographer. Naipaul seems to be free in his movements, independent in the way he approaches persons and events and guided only by his own sympathies free of constraints.

Naipaul's life as a travel writer began when he was twenty-eight and toured the Caribbean for a project on European colonialism in the Caribbean and Latin America. Years later he remarked that he wrote more romantically then than he really felt and that he repressed his fears. He only saw what was acceptable and pleasant for him. During his voyages to Africa, however, he reflected his motives and secret fantasies right from the beginning. He confesses with surprising frankness that he wanted to experience France in Africa, that he was intrigued by the idea of hearing the French language spoken by Africans and drinking French wine in a tropical street café: "France in Africa: I imagined the language in the mouths of elegant Africans; I thought of tall, turbaned women, like those of Mali and the Congo; I thought of wine and tropical boulevards" (*Centre* 79). Exoticism makes way for the lived experience of a fragmented and syncretistically mixed world composed of tradition and modernism. But Naipaul sticks to his beliefs as if living in a self-written novel.

Again one could search for autobiographical details in his latest, slim novel *Half a Life*, but it would be more appropriate to look out for literary influences, such as that of William Somerset Maugham, in whose *The Razor's Edge* the American Larry seeks enlightenment in colonial India. He meets a brahmin who left his secular life behind in order to devote himself to silence and asceticism. When the American touches the brahmin he feels a divine inspiration. He returns happily to Illinois to live in "calmness, forbearance, compassion, selflessness and continence" as a cab driver (*The Razor's Edge* 306).

The beginning of *Half a Life* is similar to Maugham's novel—the only difference is the fact that Naipaul introduces farcical elements and tells the story from the brahmin's point of view. In this version, however, there is no place for abstinence and spirituality. Willie's father, who has heard about Gandhi's teachings and the Mahatma's idea of crossing the whole of India on foot in order to harvest salt by the ocean, wants to accomplish something similarly splendid, "following the mahatma's call" (*Half a Life* 20). Consequently, the father, who remains nameless throughout the novel, marries a woman from the lowest caste: "This was the girl I thought I should go and make a declaration to and in her company live out a life of sacrifice" (*Half a Life* 13). Throughout his life he regards this decision as a magnanimous deed—however, the dark-skinned woman he marries, Willie's and his sister Sarojini's mother, he despises whole-heartedly. Out of laziness and foolishness the father destroys files at his office and declares this sloppiness to be a heroic moment of civil disobedience against himself, a moment Gandhi would be proud of.

Already in *An Area of Darkness*, his first book on India, Naipaul describes with mocking ire how Gandhi's work was destroyed by his Indian compatriots in that they made him a saint and reinterpreted his teachings into convenient and domestic use. *Half a Life* picks up this aspect in quite humorous form when Willie's father does not confront Gandhi's quest as to how to live one's life, but only pragmatically and coolly watches out for what would be easiest to give up. When legal problems arise out of his professional misconduct, the father finds refuge in a temple and takes a vow of silence. There he meets Somerset Maugham, who is impressed by this man, who apparently lives composedly in his silence but in reality is only a cunning bluffer.

The boy Willie discovers his passion for writing while in a

missionary school and constantly invents new parables about mendacious kings and brahmins eating children. Upon receiving a scholarship he flees the narrowness and hypocrisy of his family and embarks on a journey to England, into the literary bohème of the late fifties, there to copy his father's behaviour with regard to constantly inventing new stories about his background. His writing produces results his life is not able to: in the moments when he borrows someone else's identities from American movies around which he creates his Indian stories, he is able to produce his best narratives.

After meeting his future wife, he accompanies her to her home country of Mozambique. A new half life—the most fascinating of this novel—begins for Willie, as his wife's appendage, as master of an estate, as the eternal stranger in a tiny oasis of leisure and luxury created in the middle of the African wilderness by Portuguese colonials:

> Looking out from the bedroom window, through wire netting and dead insects, at the rough garden and the tall paw-paw trees and the land falling away past groves of cashews and clusters of grass roofs to the rock cones which in the distance appeared to make a continuous low pale-blue range, Willie thought, 'I don't know where I am. I don't think I can pick my way back. I don't ever want this view to become familiar. I must not unpack. I must never behave as though I am staying' (*Half a Life* 126).

The once mercilessly sarcastic Naipaul has become lenient. More than forty years ago, he prefaced *The Middle Passage* with a few brutal words from the English colonial traveller James Anthony Froude: "There are no people there in the true sense of the word, with character and purpose of their own." In *Half a Life*, Naipaul seems to have reversed this. After his flight from Mozambique, just shortly before the colony collapses and civil war breaks out, Willie tells his life-story to his sister in Berlin. It is the story of a man with a weak character and without a goal in his life. But at least he tells the story in his own words; and

Naipaul allows his sad protagonist a few cheering sexual experiences and two years during which he loved his wife Ana.

Works Cited

Maugham, William Somerset. *The Razor's Edge.* Garden City, NY: Doubleday, 1944.

Naipaul, V.S. "Two Worlds: Nobel Lecture, 7 Dec. 2001" <www.svenskaakademien.se/HTML/nobelpriset/2001/Nobellecture/n101vsne.html>.

____. *Half a Life.* New York: Knopf, 2001.

____. *Beyond Belief: Islamic Excursions Among the Converted Peoples.* New York: Random House, 1998.

____. *A Way in the World.* 1994. New York: Vintage, 1995.

____. *Finding the Centre: Two Narratives.* New York: Knopf, 1984.

____. *Among the Believers: An Islamic Journey.* New York: Knopf, 1981.

____. *The Return of Eva Peron.* New York: Knopf, 1980.

____. *An Area of Darkness: An Experience of India.* 1964. New York: Penguin, 1968.

____. *The Middle Passage.* 1962. New York: Penguin, 1969.

Special note: I would like to thank Bruce King for his advice and my wife, partner, and friend Charlene for her patience—Harald Leusmann.

6

V.S. NAIPAUL'S VULCANIZATION OF TRAVEL AND FICTION PARADIGMS

SERAFÍN ROLDÁN-SANTIAGO

The general view holds that 'travel' narratives are objective and scientific, and that they faithfully represent geographical, historical, and social reality. Of course, this is a totally false notion because travel narratives are embedded with fictional elements and figures; likewise, fiction includes many 'travel' constituents and styles, and both deal with representations that are many times exaggerated and inexact, sometimes slurred and grotesque. This is true of many types of written discourses, such as, historical writings, investigative journalism, political treatises, and natural history writings. Dissayanake and Wickramagamage point out: "[...] the distinction between fiction (created) and travel writing (factual) is a false one but also points to the misrepresentation, distortion, orientalisms, and search for cheap effects that characterise much travel writing."[1] This argument centres around the notion that 'Western' travel writing is geared to notions of colonial narratives, and its quest for representing the 'other' in postcolonial societies, and it does this by referencing the 'other' in relation to the metropolitan centre. But what is interesting is the categories and kinds of 'travel' writings that these critics identify.

Dissayanake and Wickramagamage point out three different types of travel writings which have been employed by writers in the past: 1) Information-Oriented, 2) Experiential (Sentimentalizing), and 3) Intellectual-Analytic.[2] The first category, information-oriented travel writing, tries to be more scientific and objective, and it focuses on geographic, mineralogical, botanical, agricultural, economic, ecological, and ethnographic details. The authorial voice is minimised, supposedly, and landscape and its description and documentation is placed in the front. Of course, there is an ever-present hierarchy of information order which, even denied, is linked to imperial power structures and the global system. The second deals with emotional sentiment and involvement; the writer goes into highly personal and emotional displays, and there is an emphasis on adventure and drama. Unlike the first type, there is a 'main character,' the traveler and his voice; he is the protagonist and primary focus, and there is a 'heroic paradigm.' Early American captivity narratives during the 17th to 19th century can be said to be 'travel' or exploration writings, and they are mostly *experiential* in nature, though some did include ethnographic and geographical information. This is also true of the westward movement narratives like the Platte River Road and the Oregon Trail narratives. Both of these types overlap at many times in the use of techniques. This experiential mode casts the author/traveler into the major role (as representative of the metropolitan centre), and the 'natives' in the role of the 'cultural other.' The third category is the intellectual-analytic, the most subjective of the travel modes, and most controversial. Dissayanake and Wickramagamage state: "This is the form of writing where the narrative emerges as a kind of intellectual social commentator." The authority is not derived from the presentation or documentation of information, but from the authorial voice, that is, "from the acuity of observations and depth of analysis." It is as if the author first sells himself and his name, then his travelogue with *his own views and in-depth analysis*. V.S. Naipaul would seem to fall into this last category, though, there are abundant overlapping instances from the other two types.

In this paper, I will endeavour to correlate V.S. Naipaul's travel writings with his fiction. In doing so, I will observe the constant feedback between both travel and fictional paradigms in his texts. It is not certain, like the proverbial chicken and the egg, which would come first: whether the fictional elements in his travel narratives, or the travel paradigms in his fiction. Both are inextricably woven and meshed together. This is especially true after *The Middle Passage* (1962), his first travel narrative. In his short preface to *The Art of Travel: Essays on Travel Writing*, Philip Dodd says about Naipaul: "[He] has increasingly preferred the travel book to the novel. Since travel writing shares *borders* with a number of other forms, including autobiography, biography and history [...]" (my emphasis).[3] But there is more than just bordering aspects; I believe that 'vulcanization' is a better defining term to describe Naipaul's newer forms of narratives, such as *The Enigma of Arrival* (1987) and, especially, *A Way in the World* (1994) and *Beyond Belief: Islamic Excursions Among the Converted Peoples* (1998). In these last narratives 'travel' and fictional elements and strategies have coalesced, perhaps vulcanized, so that one is presented with newer ways of textualizing social, historic and natural realities. In what way(s) are Naipaulian fictional elements such as imagery and its picaresque sense, landscape, themes, etc., transferred, perhaps transmuted, into his travel writings? And in what way(s) are his travel paradigms (specific styles and forms) transferred into his fiction? These are some of the issues that I will explore in this paper, including Naipaul's emergent philosophical ideas and perspectives.

The *objective* of travel writings has been, much like the *objective* of anthropological and ethnographic field work reporting,[4] the faithful portrayal of the 'other,' that is, the third world, marginal groups like ethnic and racial minorities (whether in the developing nations or the first world), and 'other' such groups. The strategies of 'objectivity' and 'relativity' have been research tools of traditional anthropology; either way one looks at it, the traveler-writer usually uses what Dissayanake and Wickramagamage call 'the colonial gaze,' looking down on these people and their landscapes, and studying, observing them as 'primitive,' or 'backward.' A similar perspective had been used by folklorists when studying the 'folk' in rural, and even, in urban settings: ethnic and minority enclaves were identified and studied as 'other.' The 'textualizing' of these travel experiences by writers have been, no doubt, conditioned by the centre ideologies that fit into the paradigms of colonizer/neo-colonizer and colonized, but which are not dealt with in this paper.

The definition and categorisation of 'travel writings' in this paper will be modified, not only to include 'travel' per se, but a wider base, as I shall later discuss, which includes landscape and people, historical commentary, autobiographical 'memories,' and philosophical ideas. In all of these as Dissayanake and Wickramagamage have noted, Naipaul's writings fit under the category of 'intellectual analytic' because 'self' intervenes vigorously and includes intellectual and social comments and analysis. Three formal aspects should be noted here of Naipaul's travel writings: 1) the Naipaulian assumptions, 2) his narrative authority, and 3) his travel strategies. All three are important in order to understand Naipaul's personal views of what a writer and his writing should strive for.

Firstly, there are Naipaulian assumptions or logistics, a considerably ordered plan that Naipaul employs which leads to the eventual text: a Naipaulian assumption, actual travel and note-taking, return to Centre (London) and pondering, re-assessments of original assumption, outlining, re-organization, re-thinking, re-invention of his travel experience, actual writing. It is important to understand that the actual travel experience *with notes* is not the final text-product; it is merely a beginning. The actual text must be produced 'in vitro,' that is, 'out of' (or separate from) the actual experiential context: it is a 'remembered' thing, accessed from both Naipaul's memory, and his travel notes and journal. But the actual product of the narrative might have different assumptions, time-space arrangement might be different, and the narrative will finally evolve into a re-invention of his travel experience. His travel narratives will, many times, move around different time/space points. And they will reflect deeper analysis from his post-travel re-assessments. A text (in the generalised definition as an 'art product') whether it is travel, fiction, history or art will always be a representation of reality. This 'representation' is a cultural product that is 'determined' by dominant ideology and worldview. What Naipaul 'saw' and observed in his travel experience is not totally represented in his travel narratives; it is a very critical selection of a reality that reflects a Naipaulian idea or perspective, a set of assumptions.

It is important to note when reading Naipaul's travel narratives that the text may have a chronological basis as one reads it, but the original Naipaulian thought (the specific spatial and temporal points) at the time of any specific scene that one reads, is not necessarily the Naipaul of that scene; it is the later Naipaul, the author who has refined his experience through writing, the one who has re-worked his assumptions and ideas, who has re-formulated and textualized his travel. The text (and Naipaul its author) *knows* the space and time (and the ideas and knowledge that this entails) of the actual travel; what Naipaul has done is to 'textualize' it, organize and represent it more efficiently according to his assumptions.

Secondly, Naipaul uses a 'narrative authority,' a way of convincing his reader/audience of his views and perspectives, a way of giving 'authority' to his travel narrative as an 'objective reality.' He convinces us by: a) giving an eye-witness experience, b) demonstrating an 'acuity of observations,' c) employing analytical skills, and d) offering us a very readable and pleasing narrative. Naipaul visited India for many months on different occasions in order to gather 'materials' for his *An Area of Darkness* (1964), *India: A Wounded Civilization* (1977), and

India: A Million Mutinies Now (1990); he also visited the Islamic world for seven months to obtain 'materials' for his *Among the Believers* (1981), and a five month journey for *Beyond Belief: Islamic Excursions Among the Converted* (1998). For the *Middle Passage* (1962), his first travel narrative, a short trip of several months was taken. Extensive travel and research were also done with his other travel narratives: *Finding the Centre* (1984), *A Turn in the South* (1989), and *The Loss of El Dorado* (1969). His travel narratives are not the results of cozy 'tourism.' They are serious undertakings that entail much thought and analysis; thus, the eye-witness account gives 'authority' to his writings. It is a first-hand account of what happened and who was involved. No one can doubt the extraordinary qualities of Naipaul's observations: they are keen, detailed and exact. Dissayanake and Wickramagamage write about his skills in observation in *Among the Believers*: "He has the well-trained and sensitive eye of the artist with which to record the breath taking beauty of these short summer landscapes in the mountainous regions of the Himalayas. His eye for the telling detail is extended to his descriptions of the people too. So it is that he manages to outline vividly a portrait of the Afghan herdsman whose manner and physique obviously intrigue him."[5] Naipaul uses sharply his analytical skills when making comments about people and situations. In *India: A Wounded Civilization* (1977) one can appreciate this keen analysis as we shall later see. The rhetorical skills of 'convincing' and 'engaging' readers is of great importance to any travel writer, even if this means 'creating' sometimes a false illusion, an illusory text that 'twists' representations of reality in subtle ways, creating many times grotesque and picaresque images.

Thirdly, Naipaul employs particular 'travel writing strategies,' that is, different techniques and approaches have been carefully manipulated: a) journalistic techniques, b) detailed ethnographic reporting, including landscape, geographic, and human observation, c) historical perspectives and style, d) autobiographical features, and e) philosophical inquiry. It is important to note that some of his travel texts completely focus on one of these paradigms, while at other times, his travel writings contain some of these together, sometimes overlapping, at other times 'blending.' Robert Nixon included a separate chapter in his seminal thesis, *The Grand Hotel Abyss: A Critique of Naipual's Third World Travels,* on Naipaul's use of techniques of travel, ethnography and autobiography, and his intensive use of these genres or styles which Nixon terms, "amateur ethnography."[6]

Naipaul uses various of these strategies to textualize his travels. Some of his travel narratives like *The Return of Eva Peron, with the Killings in Trinidad* (1980)[7] apply mostly one strategy, in this case, the journalistic technique. It consists of four pieces, three of which (except 'Conrad's Darkness' which is more philosophical and literary) are formally speaking, investigative journalism. Naipaul has employed a pithy and factual style, a prose which readers will not find cumbersome. He has documented his writings with actual court transcripts (the 'Michael X' narrative), very detailed and graphic, and he has also included newspaper articles, and historical documents. *REP* represents a thorough and total investigative journalistic narrative. These journalistic techniques of gathering and presenting facts, figures and dates abound in all of his travel narratives. The fresh and uncluttered phrase reminds one of clear first-rate journalistic writing.

Naipaul is also known for his accurate ethnographic observations; he has an eye for exact ethnographic detail. It is wrought out and produced by a 'detached' and clinical perspective, reminding one of anthropological reports and ethnographies, though the full ethnographic depth may be lacking. Using this writing strategy, Naipaul includes such descriptions and observations as landscape, topography, and people. The last are depicted, many times because of this cold 'detachment,' as mere objects and not humans. This is a setback of this ethnographic method, because 'colonial gaze' is usually used. In most of his travel narratives this 'ethnographic' style brings 'narrative authority' to bear.

Naipaul also includes in many of his texts historical research, and proper documentation and style. *The Loss of El Dorado: A History* (1969) represents a truly interesting and historical treatment of Caribbean history centring around the specific theme and myth of 'El Dorado,' the South American city of gold. In this narrative Naipaul uses British travel reports and early histories from the 17th to 19th century on the Caribbean. This text represents another example in which one of these strategies, the historical perspective, is integrated totally in the narrative. It is an example of a thoroughly and scholarly documented piece of writing which may give Naipaul's readers an interesting perspective about his other historical side. Naipaul states in the first lines of the "Postscript": "This *narrative was structured* mainly from documents—originals, copies, printed—in the British Museum, the Public Record Office, London, and the London Library" (my emphasis). These historical techniques are also included, partially, in travel texts such as *The Middle Passage* (1962), *An Area of Darkness* (1964), and *Among the Believers* (1981), and fully integrated in his experimental and most recent narrative forms, *A Way in the World* (1994), and *Beyond Belief* (1998). Naipaul weaves into his travel narratives strands of historical writings and quotations of passages, thus, enforcing and giving additional 'narrative authority' to his writings. Traditionally, historical writings were characterised as 'objective,' 'factual,' and 'authoritative.' At least, this is the perspective and value judgement that many casual readers give to historical writings without taking into account the various types of discourses and ideologies. But Naipaul adds his own personal dimension to many 'historical' passages. Subramani comments on *The Middle Passage* with its synchrony, and *The Loss of El Dorado* with its diachronic historical perspective: "Together, these two books constitute a penetrating and comprehensive analysis of the socio-historical predicament of the West Indies. They also provide some unsettling insights into the colonial process."[8] Naipaul has employed historical perspectives along with personal ideas about the Caribbean in both his fiction and travel narratives: "No discussion of his works can ignore the historical dimension, which is inseparable from the philosophical artistic dimensions [...]. Man's homelessness is not an external fate: Naipaul attributes it to concrete historical circumstances. Naipaul often finds the plots for his novels in history, and the dramatic actions flow from the conflict between character and historical circumstances."[9] This is especially true in *A Way in the World* (1994) in which history is intricately woven with fiction. Naipaul has artistically meshed together literature and history, e.g. dialogue, characterisation, techniques of narrative, and the historical perspectives of time and space. As Subramani has concluded in relation to *The Loss of El Dorado*: "Naipaul has combined the apparently dichotomous task of the historian who depicts individuals to illuminate historical process or historical period, and the novelist who is interested in individual psychology and morality."[10] This will be of utmost importance in Naipaul's later works in which total vulcanization has taken place.

Nightingale also notes a similar relationship between *MP* and *The Loss of El Dorado* in terms of their 'historical' perspectives.[11] This Naipaulian historicity is very functional as narrative technique in both his fiction and travel writings: "To Naipaul the study of history offers more than a personal haven, a way of holding the vision of chaos at bay. It also offers to a society a means of establishing identity, through a shared heritage, the development of mutual ideals and a sense of community."[12] *The Loss of El Dorado* for Nightingale is an attempt to "put the past back into a book, but not into a history textbook; rather, from scholarly research into archives, and from the author's own translations emerges a novelist's interest in characters."[13] Thus, one comes across the various travel and fictional characters, even travel contacts and informers, that form an important part of his travel narratives, especially in his latest hybrid fiction.

Naipaul's philosophical techniques are also of importance. Even though he has not produced a 'philosophical' narrative per se, it is interesting to note that the sprinkling of philosophy into his narratives have given them added philosophic 'authority.' He has embedded into his travel narratives this 'philosophical perspective.' In his autobiographically spaced "Prologue to an Autobiography" in *Finding the Centre* (1984) nothing is philosophically stated outright, but it is implied: a philosophical aura permeates this short narrative transporting one to the past with just an idea, a thought, a possibility of capturing the essential, the basic spark of experience and life. In his fiction the philosophical idea abounds everywhere: existentialism, individualism, and the concept of the 'self.'[14]

In *An Area of Darkness* the quest for the 'self' is notable: there is an intense preoccupation with the self, and this colours all of Naipaul's observations and comments. The narrative is replete with confessional statements, with philosophical commentaries, his own fears and anxieties about India. The philosophical perspective is everywhere imbedded in both of Naipaul's fiction and travel narratives; it is this *substantive-idea* that permeates his writings, and is at times connected with the 'autobiographical' sense. In fact, it will be important to add, as Niven has noted, that Naipaul has included in all of his writings, autobiographical features which many times are fused into his narratives.[15] It seems that in many passages *philosophical ideas are brought out through autobiographical instances.* Thus, one can discover a philosophical idea behind Naipaul's argument when discussing 'Conrad's Darkness': "In the experience of most writers the imaginative realising of a story constantly modifies the writer's original concept of it. Out of experience, fantasy and all kinds of impulses, a story suggests itself. But the story has to be tested by, and its various parts survive, the writer's dramatic imagination."[16] To summarise, Naipaul's travel narratives are replete with these writing strategies, their main function being to enhance and convince the reader of the 'idea' or 'mood' which needs to be communicated, and at the same time, invoking some form of 'narrative authority,' not to mention his intense exploration of 'self.' Let me briefly pause to discuss Naipaul's most important fictional components so that I may explore the dynamic interrelationship between both his travel and fictional writings.

Naipaul has included in his fiction since the early Trinidadian novels prior to *The Middle Passage* certain fictional elements that are crucial to him. First of all, he has dealt with themes of poverty, desolation, decay and decadence. Since the beginning, Naipaul has sought for a sense of unity, rationality and self-awareness; this has been coupled with his quest for order. Everything which implies disorder and irrationality has made Naipaul feel uncomfortable and bothersome: the sense of order, the cleanliness, the logical and rational, the quest for individuality have been basic tenets that he has explored in his writings. He has been constantly trying to make order out of chaos, that is, 'textualizing' these ideas, and his travel experiences and fiction. For Naipaul 'textualizing' has meant putting 'order' to things. This sense, of course, has spread into two areas in his writings: imagery and tone. In his early fiction there were images of people, places and landscape, which at the time, were not totally engrossed or engulfed by serious tone, but were lighthearted and humorous, such is the case in *Miguel Street, A House for Mr. Biswas, The Mystic Masseur* and *The Suffrage of Elvira.* The use of imagery as part of the narrative begins to be applied more fully in *A House,* but there are passages in *Miguel* and *Mystic* which include somewhat developed imagery and landscape. The third Naipaulian element that needs to be addressed is tone. Here Naipaul takes us on a trip amongst shades of irony that range from humorous light-hearted irony, somber, serious irony, satire, cynicism, sarcasm, and sometimes mockery. Again, the humorous irony was frequently used in these early Trinidadian narratives. Nixon has characterised the earlier fictional tone of Naipaul as 'often empathetic satire' as opposed to *MP*'s later 'relentless negativity.' The critic also labeled it as "a purgative journey of rage into the terra incognita of the self," which is putting it very bluntly to say the least.[17] All three of these Naipaulian fictional elements—theme, imagery and tone—have been carried over into his travel writings, including characterisations, and use of dialogue.

It is important to note that his first travel narratives, *The Middle Passage* (1962), and *An Area of Darkness* (1964) were published between his early Trinidadian novels, from 1957 to 1961 and his later fiction, *The Mimic Men* (1967), *A Flag on the Island* (1967), *In a Free State* (1971), and *Guerrillas* (1975). There is a marked difference between his early and later fiction prior to *The Middle Passage* and *An Area of Darkness.* One can already identify certain strategies in both travel and fiction which were being carried over in both directions. *The Loss of El Dorado* (1969), a historical monographic essay which added scholarly zest to the Naipaulian canon, was published between *The Mimic Men* and *In a Free State.* After the publication of *India: A Wounded Civilization* (1977) and the essays in *The Return of Eva Peron, with The Killings of Trinidad* (1980), that were researched and published individually before 1980, the great novel, *A Bend in the River* (1979) was published at the height of this Naipaulian dynamic-feedback between his travel and fictional writings. The text, *A Bend,* represents a state of maturity between travel and fictional writings; indeed, *A Bend in the River* is the last novel that Naipaul has written which can be strictly labeled as 'novel.' After *A Bend* his narratives have been oriented towards 'travel' with texts such as, *Among the Believers* (1981), *Finding the Centre* (1984), *A Turn in the South* (1989), *India: A Million Mutinies Now* (1990) and *Beyond Belief: Islamic Excursions Among the Converted Peoples* (1998). But it is the early *MP* and *An Area of Darkness* which greatly influenced his later fiction.

Naipaul's early fictional elements, not highly developed at the time, were the ironic tone, the sharp image, and the themes of futility, inability and frustration. The use of the ironic tone can be seen in his first two written works, *Miguel Street* and The *Mystic Masseur.* A few passages are given below:[18]

> Then the war came. Hitler invaded France and the Americans invaded Trinidad. Lord Invader made a hit with his calypso [...]. For the first time in Trinidad there was work for everybody, and the American paid well (*MM* 141-42).

> Every Saturday evening the men gathered in Beharry's shop and drank a lot of bad rum. They became sufficiently enthusiastic about their wives to beat them that night. On that Sunday they woke sick, cursing Beharry and his rum, continued sick all day, and rose fresh and strong early Monday morning, ready for the week's work (*MyM* 64).

> He had never before realised that paper could be so beautiful, that there were so many kinds of paper, so many colours, so many glorious smells. He stood still, marveling and reverent, until he heard a woman's voice (*MyM* 76).

Now let us compare this lighthearted humorous tone with his later tone in *The Mimic Men* and *In a Free State* which is infinitely more pessimistic, ominous and threatening:

> To be born on an island like Isabella, an obscure New World transplantation, second-hand and barbarous, was to be born to disorder (*MM* 118).

> We pretended to be real, to be learning, to be preparing ourselves for life, we mimic men of the New World, one unknown corner of it, with all its reminders of the corruption that came so quickly to the new (*MM* 146).

> Linda said, 'Now I imagine he's going to telephone his other fat friends, and they'll be waiting for us at some roadblock. I imagine he's running to beat out the message on his drums right at this moment' (*IFS* 209).

> 'Those soldiers [Linda said] knew what they were grinning about. Did you see them grinning? Savages. Fat black savages. I can't bear it when they grin like that' (*IFS* 214).

Certainly the tone has changed since *Miguel Street*; also one can see imbedded very firmly this new tone of extreme pessimism in his travel narratives. The sharp literary image is also important and crucial in Naipaul's fiction. Only a few instances of landscape imagery and ethnographic detail especially when he describes people and places will be given. But his early images are almost void of tone; his later images are permeating with Naipaul shades of bitter irony and satire. In *A House for Mr. Biswas* an image was produced of a black woman who lived in a shack. Notice the sharp ethnographic detail imposed; and also the detail description of the 'little cemetery.' These images are very objective and contain very little 'personal' comment as seen through the use of tone.

> From the shack in the hard yellow yard a Negro woman came out, a large calabash full of corn in one hand. Her tight cotton dress imperfectly covered her big body and her kinky hair was in curlers and twists of newspaper (*AHB* 238).

> Mr. Biswas waved at the forlorn little cemetery and the dirt lane which, past a few tumbledown houses, disappeared behind bush and apparently led only to more bush and the mountains which rose at the end (*AHB* 396).

Naipaul begins to use vivid and long description in *A House for Mr. Biswas*. His early novels prior to *A House* generally consisted of more dialogue and less narrative. When writing *The Mimic Men*, Naipaul had already produced two travel narratives. One cannot but notice the difference in imagery that he uses. His travel paradigms have finally been incorporated into his fiction. No doubt, he had obtained 'materials' from his *The Middle Passage* and *An Area of Darkness*.

> We drove along narrow rough roads into the valleys of our eastern hills. We went through purely mulatto villages where the people were a baked copper colour, much disfigured by disease. They had big light eyes and kinky red hair. My father described them as Spaniards. They were a small community, exceedingly poor, separate even in slave days

> and now inbred to degeneracy, yet still distinguished by an almost superstitious fear and hatred of full-blooded Africans and indeed of all who were not like themselves (*MM* 121).

> A charcoal burner had found the animal, garlanded with marigold and faded hibiscus, on a freshly prepared platform of beaten and plastered earth. Heart and entrails had been torn out; but there were flowers on the animal's mane. Flowers woven into its tail; and the coat had been brushed as though by proud grooms (*MM* 140).

These passages are part of a novel not a travel narrative, but they may confuse the reader because they seem to be extracted from a national geographic or some other travel magazine. The ethnographic detail and narrative texture is convincing and realistic. One can appreciate the influence that 'travel' has had on his fiction.

Naipaul has always been interested in the grotesque and picaresque images, and these have also been incorporated in both his fiction and travel narratives.

> Something was wrong with Carter's molars, and he ate like a dog, holding his head over his plate and catching the food in his mouth with every chew, at the same time giving a slight hiss, as though every mouthful was too hot (*IFS* 134).

> The Africans had never been easy to see, with their black skins and multi-coloured cottons. And now Bobby and Linda saw that the hillside along which they had been driving was alive with Africans. Wherever they looked they saw more. On a wide ledge cut into the hill was a low thatched shelter. With its rough leaf-thatch and black poles, trimmed tree branches, it has at first looked just like a part of the woods; but it was packed with seated Africans, all in new clothes (*IFS* 164).

> At a twist in the road ahead, where the bare verge widened and rose and fell away, half a dozen small domestic animals

> stood together silhouetted against the sky. But two turned out to be naked children. Dull-eyed, disfigured with mud, they stood where they were and watched the car pass (*IFS* 205).

These images were taken from *In a Free State*; they are grotesque representations, caricatures, with cynicism and satire. It should be noted that Naipaul is not solely content with using 'objective' images, but 'anointing' them with the Naipaulian dark ironic and sarcastic tone. His images are stark, naked, compulsive, threatening, gross, brimming with irony, and highly stylised; nevertheless, they are extraordinary and extravagantly wrought out. Finally it is in *Guerrillas* and in *A Bend in the River* that the totally grotesque images are interwoven in the texts, bringing about images that were probably acquired during travel, but transformed into a Naipaulian poetics of dissolution and decadence. The themes of decay and futility that were with him since the beginning are now vividly portrayed by manipulating both tone and imagery into his fiction.

> Past the junked cars in the sunken fields, past the factories, past more country settlements, the suburbs, they approached the city, the rubbish dump smoking yellow-gray, the smoke uncoiling slowly in the still afternoon, rising high and spreading far, becoming mingled with the pink pall from the bauxite loading station, the whole shot through with the rays of the declining sun (*GUE* 163).

> There was a latrine smell, which became sharper. The latrine with corrugated-iron walls and road and a sagging, open corrugated-iron door, stood on a rough concrete foundation just outside the bush, in direct sunlight. Brilliant green flies buzzed about it and within it, striking the corrugated iron (*GUE* 237).

> In the forward part of the steamer, beyond the second-class w.c.s., water always running off their steel floors, and in the narrow walk beside the cabins, among the defecating

> babies, the cooking and the washing and the vacant girls being intently deloused, in a damp smell of salted fish and excrement and oil and rust, and to the sound of gramophone records, there are stalls: razor blades, batteries, pills and capsules, soap, hypodermic syringes, cigarettes, pencils, copybooks, lengths of cloth [...] *these are the products of the outside world that are needed; these are the goods for which such exertions are made* (*ABR* 183-84).

> Basins of grubs and caterpillars; baskets of trussed-up hens, squawking when they were lifted by one wing by the vendor or a prospective buyer; dull-eyed goats on the bare, scuffed ground, chewing at rubbish and even paper; damp-haired young monkeys, full of misery, tethered tightly around their narrow waists and nibbling at peanuts and banana skin and mango skin, but nibbling without relish, as though they knew that they themselves were soon to be eaten (*ABR* 159).

Guerrillas and *A Bend in the River* were written after his most important travel narratives up to and including *The Return of Eva Peron, with The Killings of Trinidad*. The last text served as source material along with his travel notes for both *Guerrillas, In a Free State*, and, to a certain extent, for *A Bend*. Since then, beginning with *Among the Believers: An Islamic Journey* through his later travel narratives, Naipaul has fully developed his fiction-travel paradigms, completely blending strategies, techniques and ideas from both types of writings. His literary images, dark ironic tone and themes have given his travel narratives the kind of literary qualities that readers enjoy. Furthermore, his travel techniques such as ethnographic detail, journalistic style, historical, autobiographical and philosophical sense, gave his fiction up to *A Bend in the River* the added punch that was needed.

Naipaul's first travel narrative *The Middle Passage* includes in seminal form all the travel writing strategies that he would later use. It will be noted that he had already integrated into his travel narrative strands of irony, the literary image, and his thematic ideas of pessimism and dissolution. A few passages from *MP* will illustrate this more fully:[19]

> Pursuing the Christian-Hellenic tradition, the West Indian accepted his blackness as his guilt, and divided people into the white, fusty, musty, dusty, tea, coffee, cocoa, light black, black, dark black. He never seriously doubted the validity of the prejudices from which he suffered, for he had inherited the prejudices of the culture to which he aspired. In the French territories he aimed at Frenchness, in the Dutch territories at Dutchness; in the English territories he aimed at simple whiteness and modernity, Englishness being impossible (*MP* 68).

> Felix, the village chief, [...] he took us to his hut. It was dark and dirty and dusty and disordered, like most Amerindians' huts. The sight of exposed food in the midst of dust and mud has the same effect on me as the screech of chalk on a board; I could scarcely stay to admire the Wai-Wait grater [...] (*MP* 103).

> So we started tramping through the hot dust. The smell of dog-dirt was inescapable, as was the sight of starved mongrels locked in copulation, their faces blank and foolish. Few of the thin children I saw were without some skin disease; one or two were deformed (*MP* 111).

> To see the Jamaica of the emigrants you have to look. And once you start looking, you can see nothing else. The slums of Kingston are beyond description. Even the camera glamorises them, except in shots taken from the air. Hovels of board and cardboard and canvas and tin lie choked together on damp rubbish dumps behind which the sun sets in mocking splendour (*MP* 216).

In the first passage above Naipaul has employed darker shades of irony and cynicism; things have changed since *Miguel Street*; there is no longer room for humour, and he is more blunt and critical. But it does offer the journalistic pithy statement, the fact and the detail. This is also the case with the last passage about emigrant Jamaica; it is condensed, short, factual and right to the point, perhaps distressing. Naipaul does not 'beat around the bush,' but 'lays it down.' Thus, the sentences are short, the ideas compact and the prose convincing. In the second and third passages Naipaul uses the ethnographic detail to highlight a situation: a native Indian hut that he visited, and a gross image of dust and dog shit. Both have been described very objectively, but with a tint of irony. Here we have in both passages journalistic reporting with ethnographic detail. The passages quoted from Naipaul's fiction (just before the *MP* passages) will, no doubt, offer comparable images to the above *MP* excerpts in order to illustrate the crossover from both the travel and fictional writings. The passages both in *Guerrillas* and *A Bend in the River* are comparable to the passages in *MP*. The mix of imagery with journalistic technique is fashioned and brought forth extremely well in *MP* as one critic has noticed: "This voice, which achieves its most powerful effects through *blending first-hand observation with illuminating imagery*, is far removed from both the manner of the Victorian traveller and the enfeebled explorer. It is a voice which is much closer to Naipaul the novelist, and it informs many of the most interesting passages in *The Middle Passage*"[20] (my emphasis).

As Thieme has noted, Naipaul employs very skillfully in *The Middle Passage* the journalistic and historical quote to enhance the authority of the narrative: "One of his ways of dealing with the problem is to interlace first-hand observation and commentary with references to earlier 'authorities.' most of them British."[21] These British 19th century sources, Froude, Trollope and Kingsley, were quoted very heavily by Naipaul, and are connected with techniques of 'narrative authority.' The use of these sources helped Naipaul not to succumb to 'naive empiricism' and simple personal recording of subjective impressions as Thieme has noted,[22] and enhanced his detachment and objectivity, that is, it gave the necessary added authority to the narrative.

When Naipaul was writing *An Area of Darkness* he had already acquired the necessary techniques in travel writing to incorporate them into his later post-Trinidadian novels, the first of which was *The Mimic Men.* One cannot but distinguish between the Trinidadian novels and his later fiction. The literary themes of desolation, and decadence, along with his shades of irony, and the sharply focused image gives his travel narratives the necessary 'literariness,' and at the same time, his travel narrative techniques give them 'authenticity.' A few passages from *An Area of Darkness* may serve to illustrate this point.

> On the train to Cairo the man across the aisle hawked twice, with an expert tongue rolled the phlegm into a ball, plucked the ball out of his mouth with thumb and forefinger, considered it, and then rubbed it away between his palms (*AAD* 14).

> Nowhere do I see the India I know: those poor fields, those three-legged dogs, those sweating red-coated railway porters carrying heavy tin trunks on their heads (*AAD* 71).

> Ten months later I was to revisit Bombay and to wonder at my hysteria. It was cooler, and in the crowded courtyards of Colaba there were Christmas decorations, illuminated stars hanging out of windows against the black sky. It was my eye that had changed. I had seen Indian villages: the narrow, broken lanes with green slime in the gutters, the choked back-to-back mud houses, the jumble of filth and food and animals and people, the baby in the dust, swollen-bellied, black with flies, but wearing its good-luck amulet. I had seen the starved child defecating at the roadside while the mangy dog waited to eat the excrement (*AAD* 48).

> Shankaracharya Hill, overlooking the Dal Lake, is one of the beauty spots of Srinagar. It has to be climbed with care, for large areas of its lower slopes are used as latrines

> by Indian tourists. If you surprise a group of three women, companionably defecating, they will giggle: the shame is yours, for exposing yourself to such a scene (*AAD* 73).

> The camp was a chaos of tents and guy-ropes and cooking stones and pilgrims defecating behind every bush. The woods were already littered with uncovered excrement; hanks and twists of excrement crowned every accessible boulder of the Lidder river, beside which we had camped (*AAD* 167).

> A child was squatting in the mud of the street; the hairless pink-skinned dog waited for the excrement. The child, big-bellied, rose; the dog ate (*AAD* 215).

All these passages include ethnographic details and literary images, written in a journalistic style and captured in time; the instance has been well preserved. In these travel passages Naipaul gives both authenticity and 'literariness' to his narrative and embeds them, of course, with his shades of ironic tone and disapproval.

The *Return of Eva Peron, with The Killings of Trinidad* consists of four essays written at different times during the 1970s. The information obtained from his travels through the Caribbean and Africa produced these essays, but they also furnished raw material for his novels, *Guerrillas* and *A Bend in the River*. As has been already noted above both "The Killings" and the Mobutu essays were researched by Naipaul using historical and journalistic sources, and he also employed, very painstakingly, original court records and transcripts. Also, his travel experiences in Africa offered him an experiential 'source.' He relied heavily on these for his fiction; notwithstanding, he added his own personal analysis and ideas. Nevertheless, these essays along with the historical-travel narrative, *The Loss of El Dorado* (1969), represent Naipaul's serious efforts in producing investigative reporting and, perhaps in a limited manner, scholarly historical analysis. There are entire passages from the Mobutu and Trinidad essays which are reproduced almost verbatim in both *Guerrillas* and *A Bend in the River.* Here is an example from the Mobutu essay: Mobutu's cap and stick, his photographs everywhere, the little green book, the radicalisation, the presidential domain, the cabine de luxe, the steamer, the university, to mention just a few; from the Trinidad essay: similar characters, situations and violent episodes, such as the murder of the white woman. The integration of travel materials into his fiction is well wrought out in these narratives.

In *India: A Wounded Civilization* Naipaul uses newspaper reports along with personal and historical analysis. This second India travel text, unlike *An Area of Darkness,* does not employ much landscape or literary imagery. Naipaul includes personal in-depth analysis: the narrative seems to be less descriptive than the other travel narratives because he analyses India's present condition and then makes social, economic and political observations. Some passages continue to deal with aspects of 'cleanliness' as in *An Area of Darkness,* but the narrative in general tends to be more analytical, and perhaps philosophical, as the following passages illustrate.

> [...] the road and the parked cars, from the denser swirl of the white-clad crowd around the Gateway of India, the air moist, the polluted Arabian Sea slapping against the stone steps, the rats below the Gateway not furtive, mingling easily with the crowd, and at nightfall as playful as baby rabbits (*IWC* 56).

> The poor are needed as hands, as labour; but the city was not built to accommodate them. One reports says that 100,000 people sleep on the pavements of Bombay; but this figure seems low. And the Beggars: are there only 20,000 in Bombay, as one newspaper article says, or are there 70,000, the figure given on another day? (*IWC* 56)

> [...] to be in Bombay is always to be in a crowd. By day the streets are clogged; by night the pavements are full of sleepers (*IWC* 55).

> Through these sections we walked without speaking, picking our way between squirts and butts and twists of human excrement. It was unclean to clean; it was unclean even to notice. It was the business of the sweepers to remove excrement, and until the sweepers came, people were content to live in the midst of their own excrement (*IWC* 68).

> While India tries to go back to an idea of its past, it will not possess that past or be enriched by it. The past can now be possessed only by inquiry and scholarship, by intellectual rather than spiritual discipline. The past is to be seen to be dead; or the past will kill (*IWC* 191).

In the first passage an ironic tone has been employed along with the grotesque image: a sewer rat can be a playful thing in India. The second passage brings to bear newspaper statistics, but take an ironic stance: Is this journalism to be trusted? A strong pungent cynicism and sarcasm continues in the third passage; probably serving as source experience for "One Out of Many." The fourth passage deals with the constant polemics of cleanliness and excrement. Notice the details brought to bear by Naipaul to vividly describe human waste: detail at its height. The last passage of *India: A Wounded Civilization* has been quoted here to illustrate more fully Naipaul's analytical mode in this particular narrative. Here Naipaul is seen as a social critic and a prophet of doom, offering possible solutions for the problem. He is a kind of voice who is interested in waking up Indians, supposedly, before it is too late.

Among the Believers: An Islamic Journey (1981) represents the first travel narrative after his most important novels, *In a Free State, Guerrillas,* and *A Bend in the River*. It represents a very important turning point in Naipaul's corpus of travel-fiction, that is, the vulcanization of both genres into one, as his later 'novels,' *The Enigma of Arrival* and *A Way in the World* will portray. *A Bend* represents his last traditional novel, and *Among the Believers,* the first travel narrative after that novel, his most crafted travel narrative in terms of integration of both types of components. His travel strategies and techniques, along with his fictional elements are fully intertwined at this point. The use of the various shades of Naipaulian irony is highly crafted. Naipaul makes *Among the Believers* an ultimate travel/fiction journey by making the travel narrative 'feel' like fiction at many places, not only by the imagery and tone, but by the intense dramatic dialogue that he uses; his interviews are transformed into fictional dialogues. As Dissayanake and Wickramagamage have pointed out,[23] *Among the Believers* is the travel narrative that Naipaul uses to advocate his theory of the 'universal civilization' which he firmly believes in. It is the mature reflections of someone who has 'fully arrived' to his Western identity. It has given him an opportunity to place and compare this Western prejudice against the alternative cultural, religious, and political ideologies offered by Islamic fundamentalism. And it is interesting to note that it coincides with the highest Naipaulian crafted travel narrative up to that time, so that a fully 'matured' Naipual has finally 'arrived,' in both his writing techniques, and in his philosophical Western orientation. In the following passages historical analysis, landscape imagery, ethnographic detail and journalistic reporting are included and exquisitely interwoven.

> There are resemblances to the Spanish conquest of Mexico and Peru, and they are not accidental. The Arab conquest of Spain, occurring at the same time as the conquest of Sind, marked Spain. Eight hundred years later, in the New World, the Spanish conquistadores were like Arabs in their faith, fanaticism, toughness, poverty, and greed. The *Chachnama* is in many was like *The Conquest of New Spain* by Bernal Diaz del Castillo, the Spanish soldier who in his old age wrote of his campaigns in Mexico with Cortes in 1519 (*AB* 132).

> These women, wives, were workers; they were beasts of burden. Like the women of the Dakota Indians Parkman saw on the Oregon Trail in 1846. But these Afghans, and all

these mountain tribes, lived in terrain that only they could master. No one could say of them, as Parkman could say of the Dakota Indians, that they were going to be wiped off the face of the earth (*AB* 187).

In the jail in Lahore—I had been told—they had put him in a cell [Mr. Bhutto] where the cruel summer sun fell for much of the day. He asked for his drinking water to be boiled; they brought him a vacuum flask of boiling water; it was evening before the water was cool enough for him to drink. He lived simply, eating one round of unleavened bread a day; but he spent two thousand rupees, two hundred dollars, every day on his fellow prisoners (*AB* 95).

It was a land of faith, but it was also a land of dust and sand and dry nostrils and nose-picking; and the peasant woman who rubbed her hand on the rail before touching her young sons' mouths with her hand, also in between scoured and scraped at her nostrils (*MP* 147).

The hot rhoti we were offered was delicious. The tent, the cooking fire, the mountains, the river, the tea, and the roti: I felt momentarily that I could surrender to the life. But was that all they were going to have, the roti and the tea? Masood asked for me, 'Only roti and chai? No tarkari? No savoury dish of vegetables or meat?' The young man laughed. 'Tarkari? Why do we need tarkari? (*MP* 184)

A donkey, followed by two or three of its tiny fellows, came into the tent to nibble at some cut grass that was possibly being saved for a more valuable animal. The father gave the donkey a loud thump on its side with his open hand. But there was no hurting intention behind the blow; the blow had been given only for the hollow, waning-off sound (*AB* 185).

Around the corner, on the pavement of the main road, were the medicine men, with their strange stock. At first I thought the heaped-up lizards were dead or stuffed, or a

> kind of sculptures. But then one lizard (or iguana) moved, and all moved; and there were eleven of them tied to a big stone, tied by the thick end of the tail or by the waist above the hind legs, all now striving to break free on the hot pavement (*AB* 157).

The first two passages are historical in nature, giving the narrative a degree of authenticity that Naipaul urgently needed. Two separate historical sources were mentioned and quoted. This Naipaulian technique goes back to *The Middle Passage* where he quoted from Froude and Trollope, and from Ibn Batuta's medieval travel accounts. In fact there are many similar descriptive passages used by Naipaul which have their antecedents in Anthony Trollope's *The West Indies and the Spanish Main* (1860) and James Anthony Froude's *The English in the West Indies, or, The Bow of Ulysses* (1888). In the third passage quoted above journalistic strategies such as, quotations from local dailies, including Mr. Bhutto's incarceration and death were also included. The last four passages are interesting because they are examples of vivid ethnographic detail: the delicious roti, the treatment of domesticated donkeys, the medicine man's quaint lizards so exquisitely described, and of course, the grotesque imagery of nose picking. In *Among the Believers* Naipaul includes specific details such as names, dates, specific places, signs, ads, images, etc. *Among* represents a treasure trove of rhetorical, linguistic and literary constituents brought all to bear on this later travel narrative. One of the most beautiful and poetic passages, as has been already noted, is when Naipaul describes in detail the beauty of the Afghan landscape and its people.[24]

Naipaul wrote *Finding the Centre* (1984) after the publication of *Among the Believers*. It took him close to two years to textualize his experiences about the Ivory Coast and Yamoussoukro. Even though Naipaul had begun to include autobiographical features in his early fiction, it was not until *The Middle Passage* that he started to employ these in his travel narratives.[25] In the 'Trinidad' section of *MP* the narrator (Naipaul) writes about the 'fear' that overcame him; the panic that was his father's legacy to him. The narrator had just arrived in Trinidad from London on a steamer: "As soon as the Francisco Bobadilla had touched the quay, ship's side against rubber bumpers, I began to feel all my old fear of Trinidad. I did not want to stay. I had left the security of the ship and had no assurance that I would ever leave the island again" (*MP* 40).[26] And he adds: "When I was in the fourth form I wrote a vow on the endpaper of my Kennedy's *Revised Latin Primer* to leave within five years. I left after six; and for many years afterwards in England, falling asleep in bedsitters with the electric fire on, I had been awakened by the *nightmare* that I was back in tropical Trinidad" (my emphasis) (*MP* 41). These 'old' fears have tormented Naipaul since his youth, and they are very well documented in *A House for Mr. Biswas*; similarly, they continue to be included in his work, *A Way in the World* where the narrator of the 'unwritten story' almost panics in the middle of the Amerindian jungle, and wants to return. An irrational 'fear' grips his soul: "It is pain rather than love which now suffuses the narrator's vision, and corrupts everything that he sees. It is all like something he has already lost: the late afternoon light, the friendly women and children, the very blue smoke. And now all the half-formulated doubts, mere impulses, of the last few days harden into a determination to turn his back on these people, to put them out of his mind" (*AWW* 66). This 'old' autobiographical fear is back to haunt Naipaul the narrator of the narrator.

In the first narrative of *Finding the Centre*, "Prologue to an Autobiography," Naipaul is totally involved in this autobiographical sense; it is the primal motive: he is documenting his early trials as a young writer. But as he states: "it is not an autobiography, a story of a life or deeds done. It is an account of something less easily seized: my literary beginnings and the imaginative promptings of my many-sided background." (*FC* vii) The autobiographical sense pervades mostly this first narrative, while journalistic comments and observations, and landscape descriptions are used in his second narrative, "Crocodiles of Yamoussoukro." Both narratives deal with the writing process: the first, with his early writing of *Miguel Street* in London, and the visit he makes to the real-life Bogart in Venezuela; the second with his travel experiences in the Ivory Coast. Dissayanake and Wickramagamage have noted that both texts are and can be considered as 'travel' writings because they deal with the notion and act of travelling; one is a journey into memory, this memory (historic and diachronic) being of utmost importance to Naipaul's writings; while the other deals with a physical journey in the Ivory Coast, and the importance of travel (spatial and synchronic) to the writer.[27]

In both narratives fictional aspects abound: characterisations, use of dialogue, tone, and imagery. Let me quote a few passages to illustrate. The vulcanizing efforts of blending both travel and fictional components in these later texts should be noted. In the "Prologue" he characterises a conversation that he had with his mother, and transforms it into a quite sophisticated fictional dialogue:

> I said to my mother one day when I came back from the Port of Spain newspaper library. "Why didn't you tell me about the sacrifice?" She said simply, "I didn't remember." She added, "Some things you will yourself to forget." "What form did my father's madness take?" [I asked] "He looked in the mirror one day and couldn't see himself. And he began to scream," [she said] (*FC* 70).

What appears is a kind of fictional dialogue in a travel narrative, a personal Naipaulian touch. In the "Crocodile" narrative there are exceptional fictional passages which need to be cited for their descriptive imagery and detail.

> In the lake on either side were the crocodiles. We saw the first just as we left the car: barely noticeable in the muddy water, a mere protuberance of eyes, until its thorny back became clear [...] then we saw eyes and thorny backs

> everywhere on the surface of the water—the thorns like the thorns on the bark of the baobab tree (*FC* 144).
>
> Later, on the other side of the causeway, there was another ritual. The older, bigger crocodiles were there, yellow, *with twisted snouts,* heavy bellies, and teeth which, when closed together, *suggested a long, jagged, irregularly stitched wound* (*FC* 145).
>
> A shout from the crowd told me that the chicken had been thrown. And when I turned I saw the bird turned to a feathery debris in the seemingly *grinning maw of one crocodile,* not the oldest, round unseeing eyes apparently *alight with pleasure,* black feathers sticking out on either side of the jaw. A moment's ingestion, and all was gone, except for a mash in the hollow of the lower jaw. The ceremony was over. The feeder, skullcapped, *prettily gowned,* took his tin and walked back, *unsmiling,* to the Land-Rover (*FC* 146).

Here we have a tightly constructed image with ironic overtones, and perhaps a bit grotesque. It is a fictional representation of an ethnographic detail because Naipaul has added certain personal touches, characterisation and subjectivity.[28] These phrases have been placed in italics. One final passage which twists reality and leaves one thinking of what might have really happened, was the instance of the "defective refrigerated container on the Abidjan docks": "[...] part of a cargo from the Ivory Coast to Nigeria—had begun to give off an offensive smell. The container had been opened; it was found to contain severed heads. *Sacrificial heads, for export; technology at the service of old worship.* Was the story true, or was it an expatriate-African joke?" (my emphasis) (*FC* 172). This semi-journalistic passage contains biting comments and sharp irony.

But it is in his latest 'novel,' *A Way in the World,* that Naipaul totally fuses both travel and fictional paradigms. It is a unique experience. Since *Among the Believers,* and his later *Finding the Centre* and *The Enigma of Arrival* (1987) Naipaul was very actively engaged in his vision of a 'new' literary genre; there were already hints at what Naipaul was doing, but it is in *AWW* that he totally fulfills his vision of the 'new' travel-fiction complex, perhaps what I have termed as *travelon*, or *novelogue*. *AWW* is an extremely confessional and personal account of travel experiences and autobiographical memories that spans Naipaul's entire writing career. It reads as a complex of travel-autobiography-fiction: all of the travel strategies mentioned above have been included, i.e. journalistic, ethnographic, historical, philosophical and autobiographical strategies, along with Naipaul's typical fictional elements of characterisation, tone and imagery. It is a narrative, in the same manner as *Finding the Centre*, dealing with the 'writer' and 'writing.' It is made up of a series of chapters or sections uniquely connected and centring around the 'writing' process: a whole chapter is dedicated to a 'narrator' and the writing of his 'text,' whatever that might be.

Historical allusions, facts, and autobiography are fastidiously intertwined in fictional passages; also, typical Naipaulian imagery abounds.

> The fires of the rubbish dump burned night and day. The smoke was black turning to dark brown; it often billowed over the highway; the smell was high; you had to turn up your car windows. The people of the shanty town, men and women and children, worked in this smoke—emblematic silhouettes—raking over the rubbish for things that could be salvaged and sold. The local corbeaux, black, heavy, hunched, hopped about the slopes of rubbish; the children of the shanty town ran between the traffic on the rubbish-strewn highway to get to the dump" (*AWW* 37).

The ethnographic detail is also fastidiously wrought out as the following passages illustrate.

> Once or twice during the day we stopped at an Amerindian village. At these village sites the river bank was higher, with a ramp or path zigzagging down to where the village

> dugouts were tied up. The people were pale, with black hair. Animated among themselves, exchanging food and goods and news, they managed at the next moment to be distant with the rest of us: holding themselves with an extraordinary stillness on their tree-shaded bank, and looking down without expression at the boat (*AWW* 46).

> Some of the women are making cassava bread. Finished rounds are on the grass roof. At the side of the Kitchen hut hangs the long plaited tube which can be twisted or wrung by means of a horizontally fitted stick, to squeeze the poison out of grated cassava: a poison caught in a wooden dish on the ground. Because this poison is valuable: it can preserve meat for up to a year (*AWW* 64).

A Way in the World is and will probably be considered Naipaul's lasting masterpiece, going beyond his early fictional narratives in terms of narrative technique and style. It is the lasting effort of an author who has been in search of 'self' as an individual and writer, even if this meant trespassing the boundaries that were fixed by traditional fiction and non-fiction. Naipaul has understood the meaning and significance of 'experience' for an author, the importance of 'translation' into words of personal and external realities. When Naipual comes face to face with an Amerindian hut and its social and natural realities an experience occurs which is mediated through a 'cultural-ideological mind.' This represents the 'first remove.' But there are other 'removes,' and most importantly, the actual textualization of that 'experience' which already has a 'remove' because it has been conditioned by a culture, a society, an ideology, and by memory. This is the problem of a writer: what he experiences has already been conditioned, idealogized, determined; now, further complication ensues when he/she is textualizing that experience. Such was the case of Naipaul and his quest for the perfect 'representation' or 'characterisation' of reality. *A Way in the World* may very well represent Naipaul's latest stage of 'involvement.'

The autobiographical sense which began to be put to use by Naipaul in his early Trinidadian novels, and his later *The Mimic Men* and *A Flag on the Island*, and in his travel narratives from *The Middle Passage* on, is now fully expressed in his latest works. Naipaul had included these autobiographical strategies in his fiction, in characters, situations, settings, descriptions and imagery; he also had used them in his travel writings, especially with the use of memory as a tool for 'genealogical' and 'historical' reconstruction. It seems to be Naipaul's quest for 'self,' his never ending search for his 'self.' He fashions his texts, both fiction and travel, by instilling or embedding 'self,' fashioning and exploring his 'self' through his writings. It is through the process of 'textualizing' that he is able to better define his 'self.' *A Way in the World* represents a text that has totally integrated the three categories discussed in this paper: the travelogue techniques, the autobiographical sense, and the fictional elements. These three areas had always seemed to be working together in Naipaul's narratives, but in his later writings, they have been vulcanized and totally integrated. It is important to note that the 'autobiographical' sense in his most recent texts has undergone an added dimension: the autobiographical sense has fused with the travel paradigms in terms of the use of 'memory' as bona-fide travel technique. Naipaul is now employing his memories to conjure up 'travel ideas' and situations, and autobiographical 'moments' of his past life and past texts in a kind of textual 'genealogical' reconstruction.

Travel and fiction narratives were produced in a parallel manner, but they are now fused, vulcanized together. These texts represent this new 'genre' paradigm, which have strong autobiographical components and rely heavily on the use of memory as valid travel paradigm. Naipual, thus, has finally developed and brought into being, what I call, his new *travelon* and *novelogue* genres with *Beyond Belief: Islamic Excursions Among the Converted Peoples* and *A Way in the World*. It would not be presumptuous to declare that the early two separate types of travel and fiction narratives that dynamically fed into each other have undergone distinct metamorphosis. On the one hand the early novels have been transformed into '*novelogues,*' in which the principal matrix is fiction, novel, but around it, Naipaul has spun the webs and techniques of travel. On the other hand, his early travel narratives have been transformed into '*travelons,*' the principal matrix being 'travel' (which would include the travel narrative strategies already discussed), and around it Naipaul has created a web of fictional constituents, such as, characterisation, dialogue, imagery, tone, and plot; what he calls in *Beyond Belief*, 'stories.' In this last travel narrative he states in the prologue:[29]

> *Beyond Belief* adds to the earlier book, takes the story on. It also moves in a different way. It is less of a travel book; the writer is less present, less of an inquirer. He is in the background, trusting to his instinct, a discoverer of people, *a finder-out of stories*. These stories, opening out one from the other, make their own pattern and define each country and its prompting and the four sections of the book make a whole (xii).

> I began my writing career as a fiction writer, a manager of narrative, at that time. I thought it the highest thing to be. When I was asked—nearly forty years ago—to travel about certain colonial territories in South American and the Caribbean and to write a book, I was delighted to do the travelling—taking small airplanes to strange places, going up South American rivers—but then I wasn't sure how to write the book, how to make a pattern of what I was doing. That first time I got away with autobiography and landscape. It was years before I saw that the most important thing about travel, for the writer, was *the people he found himself among* (xii).

> So in these travel books or cultural explorations of mine the writer as traveler steadily retreats; the people of the country come to the front; and I become again what I was

> at the beginning: a manager of narrative. [...] looking for the story [...] (xii).

His last travel narrative thus represents his latest maturation of the travel genre. Naipaul is not describing just the landscape and adding historical and journalistic facts and details. He is a 'finder-out of stories,' an author in search of characters, dialogues and situations. But notice that these stories must be faithful and not just imaginary put-ons: "[...] *it would have undone the point of the book if the narratives were falsified or forced*" (my emphasis). The old story is back: Naipaul is finding 'fiction' in reality and personal experiences. The *travelon* and the *novelogue* seem to have been Naipaul's life-long ordeal of finding 'self' in his writings; the author and the narrative voice have been, paradoxically enough, both distanced and elegantly fused together. And both have been so heavily sprinkled and embedded by the autobiographical elements that this point in Naipaul's life seems to be the beginning, perhaps, stretching it a bit, of an organized system of philosophical ideas.

Finally, the purpose of this paper was not to 'denounce' Naipual's travel narratives as 'figments of the imagination,' as 'colonial narratives,' with totally 'false representations' of social reality, as we pointed out in the first few paragraphs of this paper with Dissayanake's comments, but it was to explore the painstaking efforts of a postmodern author who has managed to integrate fiction and travel, to vulcanize both these genres into a newer form of literary discourse that explores his own peculiar sense of 'self,' worth and identity, even though this may mean to some, 'Western' absorption, or as Naipaul himself has characterised it, 'universal civilization.' It has been the quest of a life-time, a journey, a travel into self, time, and space, in which Naipaul, the author, the protagonist, the narrative voice, and the principal character have blended together, have coalesced. For Naipaul writing and textualizing is not a part-time job, it is a life-long endeavor, a quest for 'self,' worth and identity. And for Naipaul, the author and humanist, the whole wide world is a fictional arena replete and bubbling over with characters and 'stories' ready to be experienced, ready to be textualized from "the people he found himself among."[30]

Notes

1. Wimal Dissanayake, and Carmen Wickramagamage, *Self and Colonial Desire: Travel Writings of V.S. Naipual* (New York: Peter Lang, 1993) 2.
2. Dissayanake and Wickramagamage 3.
3. Philip Dodd, preface, *The Art of Travel: Essays on Travel Writing* (London: Frank Cass, 1982) vii.
4. Marcus and Fischer says: "[...] ethnography has developed a particular (and from a literary standpoint, narrow) kind of realism, tied to the dominant historic narrative motifs in which it has been framed. Ethnographies as a genre had similarities with traveler and explorer accounts, in which the main narrative motif was the romantic discovery by the writer of people and places unknown to the reader [...] it also attempted in its scientific aims to distance itself from the traveler's account and the amateur ethnographer." In George E. Marcus and Michael M. J. Fischer, *Anthropology as Cultural Critique: An Experimental Moment in the Human Sciences* (Chicago: U of Chicago P, 1986) 24; this work is of utmost importance because it gives us the theoretical perspective of modern anthropology and the "textualization" of ethnographic fieldwork among non or semi-literate peoples around the world.
5. Dissayanake and Wickramagamage 84.
6. Robert Nixon, "At the Generic Crossroads: Travel Writing, Ethnography and Autobiography," *The Grand Hotel Abyss: A Critique of Naipaul's Third World Travels*, diss., Columbia U, 1991.
7. V.S. Naipaul, *The Return of Eva Peron* (London: Andre Deutsch, 1980); further reference abbreviated as *REP*.
8. Subramani, "Historical Consciousness in V.S. Naipaul," *New Literature Review* 15 (1988): 22.
9. Subramani 29.
10. Subramani 31.
11. Margaret Nightingale, "V.S. Naipaul as Historian: Combating Chaos," *Southern Review* 13.3 (1980): 239-50.
12. Nightingale 241.
13. Nightingale 241.

14. See the following articles which deal with existentialism in Naipaul: Nan Doerksen, "In a Free State and Nausea," *World Literature Written in English* 20.1 (1981): 105-13; T. Vijay Kumar, "Being, Nothingness, and the Paradox of Freedom: A Study of V.S. Naipaul's 'One Out of Many,'" *The Literary Endeavour* 4.3-4 (1984): 8-14.

15. Alastair Niven, "Crossing the Black Waters: N.C. Chaudhuri's *A Passage to England* and V.S. Naipaul's *An Area of Darkness*," *Ariel* 9.3 (1978): 34; Niven notes: "[...] all V.S. Naipaul's prose contains a major element of autobiography even when it is the subjectivity of detached observation."

16. V.S. Naipaul, "Conrad's Darkness" in *REP* 222.

17. Robert Nixon 82, 122.

18. The following fictional works: *Mystic Masseur, Miguel Street, The Mimic Men, In a Free State, A House for Mr. Biswas, Guerrillas, A Bend in the River, A Flag on the Island, A Way in the World* have been abbreviated as: *MyM, MS, MM, IFS, AHB, GUE, ABR, AFI, AWW* respectively.

19. *Middle Passage, An Area of Darkness, Among the Believers, Finding the Centre, India: a Wounded Civilization, Beyond Belief* have been abbreviated as *MP, AAD, AB, FC, IWC, BB*.

20. John Thieme, "Authorial Voice in V.S. Naipaul's *The Middle Passage*," *The Art of Travel: Essays on Travel Writing*, ed. Philip Dodd (London: Frank Cass, 1982) 148.

21. Thieme 143.

22. Thieme 144.

23. Dissayanake and Wickramagamage 73-74: "Among the Believers as the reflections of a writer who has arrived at the most mature comprehension of his identity to date, by identifying unambiguously with his post-Enlightenment heritage and discursivity."

24. *AB* 180-203 in the chapter, "In the Kaghan Valley."

25. It is important to note that Naipaul has consistently used throughout his career as a writer, in both his travel and fictional narratives, the personal autobiographical features and "sense." But it finally explodes in his latest "fiction," *The Enigma of Arrival* and *A Way in the World*.

26. The fear is also described by Frank in *A Flag on the Island*: "Now as we moved into the harbour I could *feel the jungle press in again*. I was jumpy, irritated, unsatisfied, suddenly incomplete. Still, I made an effort." In V.S. Naipaul, *A Flag on the Island* (New York: Penguin, 1982) 124.

27. Dissayanake and Wickramagamage, chap. 5, "Discursive Space and Self-Fashioning."

28. Naipaul's conversation with Arlette at the end of the "Crocodile" narrative leaves one wondering how a factual conversation has been transformed into fictional dialogue. It echoes many characters in Naipaul's later fiction after the Trinidadian novels, and also Arlette is used as a human foil through whom Naipaul makes known his personal arguments.
29. V.S. Naipaul, *Beyond Belief: Islamic Excursions Among the Converted Peoples* (New York: Vintage, 1999).
30. The following editions of V.S. Naipaul's narratives were used: *A House for Mr. Biswas* (New York: Penguin Books, 1992); *The Mystic Masseur* (New York: Heinemann, 1971); *Miguel Street* (New York: Heinemann, 1980); *The Middle Passage* (New York: Vintage, 1981); *An Area of Darkness* (New York: Macmillan, 1965); *The Mimic Men* (New York: Penguin Books, 1975); *In a Free State* (New York: Penguin Books, 1981); *Guerrillas* (New York: Vintage, 1990); *Among the Believers* (New York: Vintage, 1982); *India: A Wounded Civilization* (New York: Vintage, 1978); *A Flag on the Island* (New York: Penguin Books, 1982); *A Way in the World* (New York: Vintage, 1995); *Beyond Belief* (New York: Vintage, 1999); *Finding the Centre* (New York: Alfred Knopf, 1984).

Works Cited

Cooke, John. "A Vision of the Land: V.S. Naipaul's Later Novels." *Journal of Caribbean Studies* 1 (1980): 140-61.

Dissanayake, Wimal, and Carmen Wickramagamage. *Self and Colonial Desire: Travel Writings of V.S. Naipual.* New York: Peter Lang, 1993.

Dodd, Philip. *The Art of Travel: Essays on Travel Writing.* London: Frank Cass, 1982.

Griffith, Glyne A. "Travel Narrative As Cultural Critique: V.S. Naipaul's Travelling Theory." *The Journal of Commonwealth Literature* 29.2 (1993): 87-92.

Harrington, Susan Tetlow. *British Writers in Tropical Africa, 1936-1985: Cultural Crossover in the Travel and Fictional Works of Elspeth Huxley, Graham Greene and V.S. and Shiva Naipaul.* Diss. U of Maryland, 1995.

Jussawalla, Feroza, ed. *Conversations with V.S. Naipaul.* Jackson, MS: UP of Mississippi, 1997.

Nightingale, Margaret. "V.S. Naipaul as Historian: Combating Chaos." *Southern Review* 13.3 (1980): 239-50.

Niven, Alastair. "Crossing the Black Waters: N.C. Chaudhuri's *A Passage to England* and V.S. Naipaul's *An Area of Darkness.*" *Ariel* 9.3 (1978): 21-36.

Nixon, Robert. "The Grand Hotel Abyss: A Critique of Naipaul's Third World Travels." Diss. Columbia U, 1991.

Rao, Susheela N. "Darkness Visible: The Emerging Portrait of India in Naipaul's Updated Indian Travelogue." *The Literary Half Yearly* 38.1 (1997): 28-41.

Subramani. "Historical Consciousness in V.S. Naipaul." *New Literature Review* 15 (1988): 21-32.

Thompson, Margaret Cezair. *Colonial Anxieties: The Psychological Importance of Place in the Writing of V.S. Naipaul.* Diss. City U of New York, 1991.

7

Better Simply to Endure[1]: Naipaul's Travels without Humour

EMILIENNE BANETH-NOUAILHETAS

In his Nobel Lecture (2001), V.S. Naipaul repeatedly refers to his childhood experience of cultural loss as a cornerstone of his identity. It is significant that, in order to evoke this cultural confusion, he insists on using the expression which he had chosen, almost thirty years earlier, as a title for his first book on India: "an area of darkness."

This darkness, to Naipaul, represents both the vagueness of all his initial knowledge concerning his origins, and the—relative—ignorance and indifference of his Trinidadian family for the world beyond their island of adoption. But it is also an area of regret, for the adult writer: a regret for a fantasy India that potentially held, as a purely virtual reality, all the answers to his questions of origin and identity; regret also, perhaps, for a time when no questions or enquiries were necessary because the Indian background was self-evident, as was the historical fact of the family's emigration: "We made no inquiries about India or about the families people had left behind. When our ways of thinking had changed, and we wished to know, it was too late" (Nobel Lecture 7).

In 1964, when Naipaul published the book resulting from his first trip to India, this nostalgia had been compounded by the stinging disappointment of his discovery of the land of his fathers: the choice of the title (*An Area of Darkness*) evokes a renewed loss—the loss of an identity that had until then been constantly fantasized as Indian. India had been, until that first visit, the comforting and imaginary cradle of 'origin,' a haven for cultural identity in the geography of his psyche. Thus at the root of Naipaul's travels on the subcontinent there is a clear longing for the recovery of a cultural, religious or historical identity. This intimate motivation taints his travelling—and his travel writing—with a very specific intention or at first a bitterness. Unable, in effect, to identify with the India he sees, and even less with Trinidad as re-examined at more or less the same period in his life (1960), V.S. Naipaul seems to anchor himself in another, unassailable, identity: that of a cynical man-without-a-country—but with more than a touch of Britishness about him, and about his language. It is indeed through the work of language in the narrative that the traveller's identity emerges (however much the narrator might seem to deny it) and anchors itself in British tradition, through a certain use of images, comparisons, clichés and irony.

I would like to examine the two early travel books *The Middle Passage* (1962) and *An Area of Darkness* (1964), which have frequently been described as "funny" or "hilarious" (notably by the publishers),[2] and discover if indeed there is any humour at play in them to counterbalance the earnestness of Naipaul's quest for origin. As a counterpoint to these two works, the account of Naipaul's visit to India (*India: a Million Mutinies Now*, 1990) confirms to what extent his travels are centred on a highly personal search for an external pattern that might buttress his intimate convictions and his perception of history, religion, and identity-forming truths. My reason for juxtaposing the two earlier works with the later one is the apparent change in the philosophy and structure of the travelling process and the issuing narrative: *A Million Mutinies* puts the emphasis on authenticity through multiple encounters with the people of India. This colossal accumulation of reported stories aims at an impression of directness, and therefore 'truthfulness,' and in this process comedy and irony have shifted, or disappeared altogether, through the narrator's efforts of empathy. But in fact, the apparent immediacy of the innumerable stories recounted in the book does not diminish the narrator's involvement, as he remains the filter of all the personal narratives, which he may choose to report in direct quotes or a biased indirect speech. The personal aims of Naipaul's travels have taken over the very structure of the work, in which he openly criticises his earlier mode of travelling: the idea that there is a 'correct' way of travelling leads directly to the illusion of a single 'truth,' and reminds me of the elusive 'real India' so often evoked in colonial writing. Why has humour failed the author in such a situation, which on the contrary should have called for an increased distance—retracing his steps, amending his previous 'rage?'

Spotting the incongruous

This is one of the most basic mechanisms of comedy: pointing out the absurd, the incongruous in otherwise familiar, schematic situations. The young Naipaul practises this constantly and savagely in *An Area of Darkness*, in precise descriptions of all the third-world quirks and peculiarities that inconvenience him throughout his tribulations.

The implicit reference to a norm—without which, obviously, nothing can be perceived as incongruous—is fundamental to Naipaul's gradual, textual definition of his identity. The silent aim, or at any rate, result, of his narrative, is to define a new origin for his voice, so vehemently non-Indian. By using irony against the object of his observation, the narrator claims a common background with his addressee, whose complicity and understanding are appealed to. It is surprising to read the Swedish Academy's account of Naipaul's art as one that "allows events to speak with their own inherent irony,"[3] when irony is a verbal construction anchored in cultural practices: in this case, the moral, cultural and scientific norms are clearly British.

As the text progresses, it becomes clear that for all his

reference to his Trinidadian childhood, V.S. Naipaul's references of normality, which he uses to underline the incongruity of Indian practices, are all, at least, Western. This is clear, for instance, in the irony with which the Indian reverence for symbolic action is denounced:

> Symbolic action: tree-planting week (seventy per cent of the trees planted die from lack of attention after the speeches), small-pox eradication week (one central minister is reported to have refused to be vaccinated for religious reasons, and vaccination certificates can be bought for a few shillings from various medical men), anti-fly week (declared in one state before the flies came), children's day (a correct speech by Mr Nehru about children on the front page of the newspaper and on the back page a report that free milk intended for poor children had found its way to the Calcutta open market), malaria eradication week (HELP ERADICATE MALARIA daubed, in English, on the walls of illiterate Hindi-speaking villages) (*Area of Darkness* 78).

Each element of the enumeration is offset by the critical comment in parenthesis, which is intended to ridicule the symbolic gesture through a silent reference to the 'norm,' i.e. the Western conception of action and efficiency. Irony functions through this shuttle between the symbol and its perceived uselessness, and also through the cumulative effect of the enumeration that transforms the incongruous into the ludicrously absurd that seems to rule all levels of action in India.

In *The Middle Passage*, the norms are even more clearly British, as the traveller-narrator first defines his identity against West Indians of every origin, then against the Dutch, the French, and even Americans. Thus the traveller leaves Martinique stating with very British contempt that he was "getting tired of the French colonial monkey-game" (218). Or even more tellingly, for it concerns language itself: "Dutch sounds so made up that at times it brings on a light-headedness in which you feel that anything said in a Dutch accent would be understood" (178). This generalisation, which rhetorically enrols the reader to the narrator's side through the use of the pronoun "you," seems to rely on a universal perception of the sound of Dutch. But such a universal perception is impossible: Dutch sounds a certain way to those who are used to certain sounds, and differently to those familiar with other sounds. However, the relativity of these perceptions is here completely ignored: in the narrator's slightly condescending, slightly amused statement, any non-English speaker can recognize the self-confidence of the native Anglophone who assumes his language is the norm. In other words, to Naipaul, and his projected reader, Dutch sounds "made up" by comparison with English, with which it actually shares many roots: but where English is the 'real thing,' Dutch is perceived as an amusing *ersatz*, an incongruity. Such examples of cultural positioning abound in both narratives.

Language is one of the points over which the narrator-traveller consistently affirms his Englishness. By painstakingly pinpointing the grammatical errors or liberties taken in local idioms, the narrator affirms in contrast the purity of his British voice. In his account of Trinidad, for instance, Naipaul interpolates extracts from the *Trinidad Guardian*, sometimes withholding all comment, as if each quotation were self-explanatory: an illustration of those Trinidadian idiosyncrasies deemed to be inherently ridiculous. For instance, this illustration of what he terms Trinidadian "Hollywood-B" culture:

> From the *Trinidad Guardian*:
>
> "CHILDREN ENCHANT AUDIENCE WITH DANCE, by Jean Minshall.
>
> This is not a review of "Dance Time 1960" which was presented at Queen's Hall on Thursday night for the first time. It is the only way in which I can show my appreciation and that of the capacity audience [sic] that was there—for an enchanted evening of purely delightful entertainment [. . .]. The dainty bridesmaids pirouetting in their rainbow

> hued ruffled tutues. Red Riding Hood and Buster Brown, and the Halsema twins as the bride and groom—how can I describe them—without repeating myself again and again?" (56-57)

The absence of narratorial comment after this gushing non-review is comment in itself—and there is no denying that the direct juxtaposition of the narrator's sober and concise style with this verbose description offers the desired linguistic contrast and draws ridicule on to the *Trinidad Guardian*. But it also suggests that this style is 'typically' Trinidadian, without justifying the claim, and especially that by opposition the narrator's English is more 'authentic.' A similar conclusion is suggested when the strangeness of an American's accent is pointed out: "'Why *thenk* you,' Mr Winter said" (153). Stigmatising the accents of the natives of a country when they attempt to speak the traveller's tongue is a frequent tactic of travel writing: it enables the traveller to assert a form of superiority over his interlocutors, and to displace the concept of foreignness: instead of being the alien in that country's culture, he presents himself as the possessor of linguistic knowledge among 'foreigners.' In other words, those with the funny accents are always the foreigners, and seldom do travel-writers reverse their point of view to examine their own competence in the vernacular tongue. But Naipaul is particularly intent on underlining specific accents: an accent is always, once again, the mark of incongruity in reference to an implied norm. By repeatedly musing on the accent of American fellow-travellers, he thus asserts his own specific Englishness: "His American accent added to the unreality of the encounter [. . .]" (152).

The same process occurs early on in *India: a Million Mutinies Now*, with, perhaps, not quite the same purpose: here the incongruous emerges when the Indian interlocutors insert English words in their speech—which, by the bye, the narrator cannot understand without an interpreter. '*Not totally*.' He spoke the words in English. With the affirmative Indian side-to-side swing of the head, he added, in English again, 'Fair' (68). Or: "He used the English words, 'love-match,' running them together and making 'love' rhyme with 'how,' so that the words seemed to have become Marathi words" (46). Here the emphasis is on the absorption by one culture of the colonial language, but the narrator also uses the linguistic process to assert his own competence as a cultural go-between. His interest has shifted, in thirty years, from proving his exteriority to India to demonstrating his relative intimacy with it: thus he also translates "proposed marriage" into "arranged marriage" (46), turning his narrative into a tentative bridge between Indian English and English English.

Thus the travel books have a clearly ontological function for Naipaul, who in finding his traveller's voice also defines his identity. First, by underlining the incongruity of certain expressions or situations the narrator uses irony to signal his own Eurocentrism and Englishness. Later, the same pinpointing of the incongruous is used to enhance the narrator's purported double cultural competence.

As incongruity is an obvious consequence of the cultural shock occasioned by travelling, one tends to expect some humour, or at least comedy, in travel writing. An expectation that is often disappointed: whenever the author lacks the inclination or the capacity to reflect on the causes of his initial shock, the incongruous can divert the narrative towards simple sarcasm, incomprehension, or indignation. The absence of comment after the long, repeated quotes from the *Trinidad Guardian*, for instance, has a sarcastic effect as the narrator thus seems to imply that they are self-evidently ridiculous.

However, in *An Area of Darkness* the narrator is from the outset aware of the possibility that India's incongruity may be linked as much to his own shortcomings as to its 'strangeness.' The possibility is merely toyed with, and hardly taken seriously, as the narrative progresses. Yet its presence allows for the successfully humorous tone of the "prelude," the first chapter, which describes the author's encounter with Bombay customs officials. The traveller's shuttling between customs offices, in search of permit after permit, all for the sake of two miserable bottles of liquor, answers Freud's description of a certain mechanism of the comic: "The answer to the question of why we laugh at the clown's movements is that they seem to us extravagant and inexpedient. We are laughing at an expenditure that is too large" (Freud 249). There is no doubt that the narrator has recognised the comic potential of the situation, and that he exploits it willingly. But humour goes beyond the recognition of the element of farce or comedy in a situation, due to excess of 'expenditure' for a given result, or the mechanisation of movements evoked by Bergson. It is the recognition that this given situation can be interpreted in quite a different way in another frame of reference: that in the comedy of Bombay customs, both the customs rules and their victim can look absurd. Such a recognition entails that the humoristic subject should acknowledge the fragility of his position and perception: which is the case for Naipaul throughout this episode.

> A transport permit was required to transport liquor from the customs to a hotel or house.
>
> "Please give me a transport permit."
>
> "We don't issue transport permits. You have to go to—." He looked up at me and his manner softened. "Here, let me write it down for you" [. . .].
>
> The taxi-driver had so far been calm; and it seemed now that my journeys had fallen into a pattern that was familiar to him [. . .].
>
> "You go," he said sympathetically. "I wait."
>
> Outside every office there was a little crowd.
>
> "Transport permit, transport permit" (18-19).

Not only comedy, but a sense of humour is evinced here because the narrator evokes the way he is seen by others, several times referring to the way he is looked at, and thus recognising how comedy can shift with the beholder.

Another rare instance of this practice of humour can be found in *A Million Mutinies*, when the author first focuses on an elderly American lady stranded in an airport: "Her eyes were now blank, as though, not through tantric excess or meditation, (which she might even have come to dabble in), but only by waiting in an Indian airport hall, she had arrived at the inner calm the famous gurus had the secret of" (138). At first the scene is close to mockery, and the narrative exploits basic comic devices, as in the irreverent juxtaposition of the spiritual and the trivial. But humour steps in when the narrator acknowledges how he was himself stunned into self-detachment after a long wait: "Indian architecture and air travel giving me, as it had given her, the Hindu idea of the illusion of things" (139).

It is easier for Naipaul to maintain that humorous, wavering perspective when observing Western travellers, with whom he identifies *in fine*, even though they may attract his sarcasm at first, than when he describes the countries he is visiting. For in his direct evocation of India, or the Caribbean, the author has too much of an axe to grind at first to maintain the relative detachment and sense of perspective necessary for the practice of humour; later, in *A Million Mutinies*, he has too much of a point to make, so that his entire narrative is constrained by a pre-determined demonstration.

Looking for patterns

It is when the various situations depicted in his first travel books are aimed at demonstrating a predetermined point that Naipaul's capacity for humour all but vanishes. The element of comedy may remain as the artist can still see how an event can be perceived comically, but the specificity of the event is too often submerged by the symbolic meaning the author wishes to attach to it. In *Area of Darkness*, the question of paperwork is once again evoked in what could be a humorous sequel to the incidents at Bombay customs that inaugurated the author's discovery of India.

> I was shouting now almost as soon as I entered government offices. At times the sight of rows of young men sitting at long tables, buried among sheaves of paper, young men checking slips of one sort or another, young men counting banknotes and tying them into bundles of a hundred, all India's human futility, was more than I could bear. "Don't complain to me. Make your complaint through proper channel." "Through proper channel! Proper channel!" But it was hopeless; irony, mockery, was impossible in India (92).

Each individual contact with public services becomes emblematic of an unacceptable, incomprehensible waste of energy and youth, just as each clerk is an embodiment of "all India's human futility." Thus every event is seen as part of a pattern which the traveller has already defined, and is given a symbolic value beyond its material significance. In terms of action, the accumulation of these encounters therefore exponentially increase the traveller's indignation, and in narrative terms, each image is transformed into a tragic metonymy which precludes any humour. The deliberateness of this process is made clear in the flat statement: "irony was impossible"—impossible because of the foreignness of the narrator's frames of reference for his Indian interlocutors. In this statement he seems to be indignantly appealing to the reader, who is supposed to share these references and therefore understand the target of such mockery. Irony is therefore replaced by violence: it could have been replaced by humour, which does not need the understanding of another party, for "it completes its course within a single person; another person's participation adds nothing new to it" (Freud 294). Indeed, humour is an effort made by the subject for himself, in order to spare himself a painful expenditure of affect. Precisely for that reason, it is shunned by the narrator who only wants to convey his indignation, and win over the reader to his cause. This is and can be achieved through mockery, as Freud explains: "By making our enemy small, inferior, despicable or comic, we achieve in a roundabout way the enjoyment of overcoming him—to which the third person, who has made no efforts, bears witness by his laughter" (Freud 147).

It is at best this type of amusement that one can derive from the highly caustic, superior tone of *The Middle Passage*. The best moments in this travel book, apart from a truly humorous episode, once again with an American fellow-traveller, in Paruima, British Guiana, are related to quotes which do indeed confirm that V.S. Naipaul has an acute sense of comedy—but not of humour. By a sense of comedy I understand the ability to point out the incongruous, whether juxtaposition of high and low references, or a mechanisation of life and processes, all seen in a set frame of reference; whereas a sense of humour relies on the ability to shift this frame of reference in order to foil emotional reactions.

When the narrator evokes an Italian co-traveller, in *The Middle Passage*, he seems to use him as a slightly ludicrous mouthpiece to offer his own opinion of their trip: "'God,' he said later, 'Ow I 'ave suffered today!'" (183) As usual, the phonetic mimicking of the Italian's accent is a light form of mockery, directed at the man's cultural identity; this amusing—and improbable—character produces a running commentary of the expedition, enabling the narrator to withhold his own comments while regaling himself with the portrait of a 'typical' Italian. That the Italian's character was established according to British clichés as soon as he presented himself in the traveller's horizon is apparent from the initial description of him: "Alberto was slender, of medium height, and his movements were of Italian 'elegance'" (179). The expression isolated by the inverted commas, meant to be transparent to a reader whose cultural categories resemble Naipaul's, is also subtly derogatory and condescending. The inverted commas imply that such an elegance is not authentic: once again, we are confronted with an implicit norm, which we can only suppose to be British. Thus when Alberto exclaims: "'I thank goodness I am Italian'" (183), he simply seems to be confirming the fatuity which the narrator has painstakingly made out as a 'national' characteristic; the events seem to be used to confirm certain predetermined 'truths.' Naipaul's talent lies in his capacity to be nevertheless amusing in reporting these details which he has already worked into a pattern, and in engaging the reader in the same process of mockery—unless he provokes total rejection. Much of his travel writing is structured in this fashion—even *A Million Mutinies*, for though the narrative there seems free, a collage of interviews, in fact all the stories presented are put together with a view to a specific demonstration.

One of the most striking and wrathful illustrations of this classification of reality into emblematic patterns, is the subject of hygiene and open-air latrines in *Area of Darkness*. The young Naipaul was clearly more than rattled by the specifics of Indian toilet habits, and he often refers to the problem. His evocation of it reaches a climax at the start of his third chapter, "The Colonial": "Indians defecate everywhere. They defecate, mostly, beside the railway tracks. But they also defecate on the beaches; they defecate on the hills; they defecate on the river banks; they defecate on the streets; they never look for cover" (70). Here the syncopated repetition of the words "excrement" and "defecate" efficiently mimic the ubiquity of the "squatting figures" denounced by the narrator: "These squatting figures—to the visitor, after a time, as eternal and emblematic as Rodin's Thinker—are never spoken of [. . .]" (70). The word is out: emblematic. But of what? The narrator grapples with this image, which, through repetition, is forced into becoming a metonymy, the essence of some truth concerning India. The comparison is laden with sarcasm: a conflation of high culture and scatology that mirrors the perceived contradiction between the Indian love for symbolic purity and material practices. But the intrusion of Rodin also confirms the traveller's exteriority as an observer, and proclaims his cultural background.

Yet the narrator attempts to assert the legitimacy of his obsession by coquettishly referring to another "anonymous" traveller, obsessed with "sanitation" (71), who also despaired of eradicating this habit. It turns out that this observer of the past is Mohandas K. Gandhi, whose vision of India, we are told, was colonial: in effect, the narrator identifies with him at least on this subject. But Gandhi is also, for most non-Indians and some Indians, an emblem of Indianness, an Indianness which the narrator sets out to deny, thus indirectly claiming a better knowledge of India than Gandhi's: "The observer is seeing what no Indian sees. But he has now declared his foreign inspiration" (71). By this account, Gandhi is displaced into foreignness, and the emblem of Indianness becomes the squatting figure: in this way the narrative first denounces a fallacy (the cliché of Gandhi as human symbol of India) and then reconstructs its own cliché. The pattern established here in support of a general "truth" ("But the truth is that *Indians do not see these squatters* [. . .]," 70) then rules both the traveller's attitude, his way of seeing, and the narrative's logic. As an observer, the traveller will classify new images according to this established emblematic value; as a narrator, he transforms experience into cliché through rhetorical short cuts: "The briefest glimpse at New Delhi's international airport is sufficient" (72). The inflated repetitions, which stylistically echo this perceived fact, "Indians defecate everywhere" (70), aim towards a comic cliché relying on a mechanisation and dehumanisation of the process. The cumulative rhetoric (the verb is used five times over four lines) is a clever comic device that maintains the narrative's seductiveness for the reader, and at the same time exploits the most childish comic pleasure of revelling in the repetition of scatological expressions.

The quest for emblematic images is much more than a simple narrative trick: it is a philosophy of travel, linked to the author's personal search for an identity. Perhaps the knowledge of the writing to come, of the narrative to construct, somehow encourages the traveller to look for serviceable vignettes which he will be able to gather under the heading of one general truth: perhaps the travel writer's vision is already intent on extracting clichés from his experience because the projected narrative structures the very process of his travelling.

Even in *A Million Mutinies,* although the project and the style of the trip itself ostensibly differ from those of the earlier books, the author cannot avoid resorting to the emblematic through his mosaic presentation of a multitude of individual stories. The idea is to offer a layered, non-judgmental and cumulative impression of a country whose complexity has to be reflected by its diversity, and in this view to accumulate exchanges with a variety of individuals from all walks of life. This mosaic effect is undeniably successful, the narrative being simultaneously fragmented through the succession of reported stories, and unified through the narrator's voice. Perhaps as a key to this unity, symbols are pointed out regularly by the traveller-narrator, as if the desire to make experience fit into some predetermined pattern of significance were his motivation. Thus a story of a life, of a person's apartment or even of their clothing, is regularly isolated by the traveller-narrator and drawn into becoming an emblem of some essential 'truth' of India—but it could as easily be humanity in general: "[. . .] I thought of the writer in his apartment: such a setting for a man who talked of his craft with so full a heart and mind, such refining of his artistic experience: such a mismatch between dreams and setting" (95). The narrator's work consists in extracting the essence of a situation, as perceived by him of course: following such a process, any scene can be an emblem of wider truths. This aim is clearly at the root of Naipaul's tribulations in *A Million Mutinies*: so intent is the traveller on this goal that humour all but disappears, and irony is repressed in an attempt to embrace all Indian 'realities' without sounding judgmental, as if to make amends for the previous approach. Indeed, some of the stories are long, direct quotations, only minimally interrupted by Naipaul's questions and sometimes even lacking any narratorial frame. But this occasional absence of commentary is not an attempt at neutrality: it suggests on the contrary that the impact of the story is self-sufficient, and enhances its symbolic, archetypal value, such is the strength of Naipaul's narrative purpose. It is an illusion to imagine that there is an irony 'inherent' to the facts: this irony can only be drawn out by the narrator's organisation of the stories collected by the traveller, and his skilful reworking of events into symbols.

Travel and earnestness

In a recent article on Naipaul, Amitav Ghosh[4] suggests that the Nobel Prize winner's style has set a standard for English travel writing, particularly in the handling of sarcasm and irony.[5] This may be the case: at any rate, another prolific travel writer, Paul Theroux, was certainly liable to be influenced by Naipaul in his early work. And there is, in *Area of Darkness* and *The Middle Passage*, such a skilful mixture of historical information, comic description and sarcastic contempt that it may come across as a tempting formula. But for all his sense of the incongruous or the outrageous, V.S. Naipaul never attempts to feign the emotional detachment that is the first stage of actual humour. On the contrary, as has also been frequently noted, Naipaul gives way to indignation or rage in his travel writing in such a way that the reader feels bullied into taking sides. In *The Middle Passage*, the narrator clearly intends to enrol the reader in his battle, through the frequent use of an inclusive "you" or "one" as substitute pronouns for the first person singular:

> Port of Spain is the noisiest city in the world [. . .]. You will realize this only after you have left Trinidad: the voices in British Guiana will sound unnaturally low, and for the first day or so whenever anyone talks to you you will lean forward conspiratorially, for what is being whispered is, you feel, very secret. In the meantime, dance, dance, shout above the shuffle [. . .]. You have been here only an hour,

> but you can feel as exhausted as though you had spent a day in some Italian scooter-hell" (50).

Here the narrator succeeds in rallying the reader's sympathy through the intimacy of the second person singular, but also by offsetting what is felt to be a shared British culture against the barbarity of the noise, which is indeed comically described (through the staple effects of mechanisation and inflation). The comparison with the Italian "scooter-hell" is one instance of the famed Naipaulian contempt, which enables him to use one cultural cliché in order to define another, while simultaneously anchoring his voice in the culture of his projected reader, who is at least neither Italian nor French. For insulting caricatures—there is also the "French flair for melodrama" (218), for instance—are not produced simply for entertainment, but to establish the position from which the traveller means to observe and speak. The accumulation of clichés concerning the Italians, the Dutch, the French or Americans, to say nothing of West Indians, rapidly makes it clear that the narrative is anchored in a British background. Naipaul's wit and use of cliché aim at creating a sense of cultural community; and Freud reminded us that "laughing at the same jokes is evidence of far-reaching psychical conformity" (Freud 203-04).

Therefore irony is not employed to diminish the narrator's emotional responses or his expressions of them—with a few exceptions. On the contrary, it is used to enhance and amplify, in the narrative, the traveller's initial shock or disgust, perhaps even to exaggerate it for dramatic effect. This reliance on affect for effect is the direct opposite of humour, which operates on a substitution of wit for distress, so that a sense of humour allows the subject to enjoy "an economy in the expenditure of affect" (Freud 293). In fact, Naipaul's main preoccupation, in the style he employs in these books, seems to be to communicate his emotions in earnest.

If it is the earnestness of the narrator's emotions that is an impediment to humour in the two earlier travel books, *A Million*

Mutinies is a different proposition. As it relies on an accumulation of reported stories, the narrative seems at first sight bent on keeping the narrator's subjectivity at bay, at dampening the opinionated passion of previous works. But we have seen how this fails, to a certain extent, as the narrator's desire for empathy is simply a new form of earnest, subjective experience. In fact, the conclusions extrapolated from some of the stories are extremely subjective, bound with the narrator's fantasies of India and its history: "I felt he was the prisoner of an Indian past no one outside could truly understand [. . .], a prisoner of India, with its multiplicity of movements and desperate needs; he could easily sink in again" (116).

Here again, the narrator's self-centredness precludes humour; it is not the self-centeredness of 'rage,' but, now, of earnest demonstration. For even before their interpretation, the stories are themselves infiltrated by the narratorial voice in the use of indirect speech, or in the manner of their introduction. This enables the narrator to mimic his position as a traveller, both present and effaced in the telling of the stories, but in the end adroitly bringing each thread together for the final spinning of his own narrative, his newly discovered "knowledge" (243) of India.

The trip, in *A Million Mutinies*, strikes me as a sort of double pilgrimage, one to observe anew, and one to write anew—a pilgrimage at the end of which a revelation was expected, as it was, unsurprisingly, obtained. "But on this kind of journey knowledge can sometimes come slowly" (243): still, come it does. It might be suggested that what Naipaul terms "knowledge" is in fact a form of subjective truth, the mythical "truth" of India which has been the object of so much wonder on the part of many European travellers. This truth of India is reinvested in the process of the author's construction of an origin, a preoccupation which he so aptly declared to be at the centre of his creative impulse, in his Nobel Lecture.

"In twenty-seven years I had succeeded in making a kind of

return journey, shedding my Indian nerves, abolishing the darkness that separated me from my ancestral past" (*A Million Mutinies* 516): the intertextual reference to *Area of Darkness* is transparent. With this last trip, Naipaul sought to construct a vision of India that would finally conform with his psychical projection of his country of origin. Revealingly, his best moment of fusion with the India he experiences as a traveller comes in one of the few flashes of humour, when he is stranded in an airport. After having mocked the vacuous expression of an elderly American, the traveller ends up in the same state and the narrator offers us some rare self-irony:

> I was taken far away from the man I had been earlier that day, and was becoming more and more like that American lady I had seen [. . .] standing rigid beside her goods on a barrow: Indian architecture and air travel giving me, as it had given her, the Hindu idea of the illusion of things (139).

This is an exact description of the state of the humorist, "taken away" from the character in command of his role. Thus if Naipaul does not consider humour an appropriate mode, it is not through lack of ability, but through a truly ideological choice in his writing and in the persona he wishes to project.

Notes

1. "[. . .] humorous books require a full life and a contented mind [. . .]. Better simply to endure." V.S. Naipaul, *India: a Million Mutinies Now* (London: Heinemann, 1990) 138.
2. On the dust-jacket of the latest edition of *The Middle Passage* (1962; London: Picador, 2001), for instance: "*The Middle Passage* catches this poor topsy-turvy world at a critical moment: a world by turns sad, earnest and hilarious—indeed, a perfect subject for the understanding and comedy of this great writer."
3. Swedish Academy Press release, 11 Oct. 2001, <www.nobel.se/literature/laureates/2001/press.html>.
4. Amitav Ghosh, *Tehelka* online magazine, 2001.
5. "It's a measure of his influence that in the West today, travel writers

are taken seriously only to the degree to which they are able to replicate the familiar Naipaulean tone of derision." Ghosh, 2001.

Works Cited

Bergson, Henri. *Le rire: Essai sur la signification du comique*. 1940. Paris: PUF, 1999.

Freud, Sigmund. *Jokes and their Relation to the Unconscious*. 1905. Harmondsworth: Penguin, 1991.

Naipaul, V.S. *An Area of Darkness*. 1964. Harmondsworth: Penguin, 1968.

——. *India: A Million Mutinies Now*. London: Heinemann, 1990.

——. *The Middle Passage: Impressions of Five Colonial Societies*. 1962. London: Picador, 2001.

——. *Two Worlds*. Nobel Lecture, 7 Dec. 2001: <http://www.nobel.se/literature/laureates/2001/naipaul-lecture-e.html>

8

V.S. Naipaul's *A Bend in the River*: Caricature as Social and Political Criticism

SERAFÍN ROLDÁN-SANTIAGO

V.S. Naipaul is well known for his incessant criticism of post-colonialism and the effect it has on the lives of the ex-colonized. He has done this by exposing in literary terms the individuals and groups who form part of the power elite in these scenarios, and who, like the "comprador," are very much a part of neo-colonialism and mimicry with its socio-cultural, political and economic platforms. These individuals and groups are held responsible for their actions and decisions. This approach gives the postcolonial writer, or in this case Naipaul, an opportunity to unmask the degenerate tyrant or neo-colonial; it gives him the chance to write, not about a romantic bliss, a heaven-on-earth situation, or some bogey folk or ethnic nicety, but about the reality of war-torn areas, political corruption, ethnic massacres, famines, economic chaos, but most of all, about self-appointed dictators and strongmen who cater to the global powers to be. Naipaul writes about leaders such as Mobutu who prefer to create artificial European cities in the middle of jungles and deserts, and who pay no attention to the real needs of the people; or like leaders in Eastern Europe, who at the end of the twentieth century, were still insisting in obliterating any opposition by any means, even if it meant murder, violence, rape, ethnic cleansing; or like some Ayatollah who prefers to insist that it is godly and morally correct to eliminate any infidel who does not agree with one's religious views, even if this means murdering, butchering or torturing the so-called unbeliever. The narrator in *A Bend in the River* makes a comment which I think is timely about the Strong Man: "[...] by-passing real Africa, the difficult Africa of bush and villages, and creating something that would match anything that existed in other countries."[1]

Naipaul brings forth his views on individual responsibility and accountability, and the fact that it must not be excused: "My attitude has always been different: that *one must look inward* and understand why one is weak [...]."[2] The critic A.C. Derrick has identified, early in Naipaul's career, a tendency to criticise the individual man: "One major thematic strand runs through all the novels [up to 1969] [...] they are satiric demonstrations *of individual* and social limitations."[3] The critic has identified an important ideological component in Naipaul's fiction, i.e. the social responsibility that has to be placed on the individual. It is not enough to say that the individual is only a product of his society; he is also a free thinking agent, capable of making decisions on his own, capable of influencing the outcome of things. Naipaul continues to believe this:

> I think there is a reason why India collapsed so easily to all these invasions and finally to the British. There is an *inward reason*. We have to look *internally* for the reason. It is not enough just to blame external forces and say the clock and the cannon, and so on. That has always been my attitude. That is the source of it. *We must examine ourselves*, examine our own weaknesses[4] (my emphasis).

Even *Elima*, the official Zaire publication at the time of this paper, stated that total blame could not be placed on the colonial past for certain things happening: "We have to understand that there is a type of underdevelopment that issues out of the habits of a people and their attitudes to life and society."[5] When you have post/colonial elite groups distorting the process of development for their own personal advantage, then, we can assuredly say that "something is rotten in the state of Denmark." V.S. Naipaul criticises and exposes these contradictions and imperial fallacies, and so becomes unpopular in the eyes of local and regional critics.

Two articles that were important in the writing of *ABR* were: "A New King for the Congo: Mobutu and the Nihilism of Africa" (1975) and "Conrad's Darkness" (1974).[6] Naipaul had written *In a Free State* (1971) a few years earlier, after a trip to Africa in 1966; and subsequently, after a similar trip to Africa in the early seventies, he wrote "A New King." This is a remarkable piece, for chunks of it are paraphrased in the novel.[7] *ABR* is a novel based on these trips to Africa and on the two essays mentioned above: The President, the Big Man, perhaps the late Mobutu, has many aspirations and dreams. He wants to build a model city (State Domain) in this African country; of course, the model is European, and that is where the problem begins. He wants an interesting combination of European 'progress' with a 'back to the African roots' component. If one compares "A New King" with *A Bend* there is no question as to the similarities, e.g. Mobutu, his cap and stick, his photographs everywhere, the little green book, the radicalization, the presidential domain, the cabine de luxe, the steamer, the university, to mention but a few.

In this same journalistic travel report, Naipaul includes many half-caricatures, that is, not full caricatures strictly speaking, but the beginnings of representations that can eventually be made into caricatures.

> In the forward part of the steamer, beyond the second-class w.c.s, water always running off their steel floors, and in the narrow walk beside the cabins, among the defecating babies, the cooking and the washing and the vacant girls beings intently deloused, in a damp smell of salted fish and excrement and oil and rust, and to the sound of gramophone records, there are stalls: razor blades, batteries, pills and capsules, soap, hypodermic syringes, cigarettes,

> pencils, copybooks, lengths of cloth [...] *these are the products of the outside world that are needed; these are the goods for which such exertions are made* (*REP* 183-84) (my emphasis).

In another passage filled with Naipaulian irony and anger at the new forms of native postcolonial relationships and attitudes, there is the following: "[...] at dinnertime in the Café de la Paix the two old men parade the young prostitutes they have picked up, girls of fourteen or fifteen. *Old men: their last chance to feed on such young blood:* Kinshasa may close down tomorrow" (*REP* 193) (my emphasis).

It is important to include at this point an observation about Naipaul's so-called journalistic pieces.[8] Some critics seem to scorn Naipaul's travels because for them, it is Naipaul's way of getting raw data for his writing, perhaps, the kind of information that tourists would look for. But this is not the case for Naipaul; he is not a tourist. It is serious business for him. He storms against critics who call his non-fiction pieces journalism. He argues that journalism is news, and he is not interested in just plain news. It is the interpretation of what happens in the world, his personal arguments and analysis that are important.

> I don't like to think of it as journalism. Journalism is news. And I don't do that. I don't write news at all [...]. My kind of writing tries to find a spring, the motive of societies and cultures, [...]. So it's that refinement of emotion that really makes the writing, what you call understanding.[9]

This paper will try to approach the specific artistic manner in which Naipaul criticises the individual person and specific groups by the use of social and political caricatures. It is an exploration of Naipaul's fictional techniques. *A Bend in the River* will be studied in terms of the use and function of caricatures as Naipaulian critical statements. In fiction many strategies can be used by writers to criticise or point out some flaw in character. The use of caricatures is one way in which an author can do this. It represents a kind of illustration in which a part, an attribute, a characteristic is made to represent the whole, of course with a slight exaggeration.

Caricatures are interesting because they can be used to reprimand some social or political situation or person, and in some countries artists and writers have even been jailed for the use of these personal metaphors. In his article "Conrad's Darkness,"[10] Naipaul tells us that Conrad used caricatures when referring to the colonials, and even, to the colonized: "Physically, he is a grotesque [referring to Karl Yundt in *The Secret Agent*], a caricature, *as are so many of the others*. For all Conrad's penetration—anarchists, policemen, government ministers."[11] The use of caricatures is of great importance as a critical method. A positive element is not caricatured; it is the negative or distasteful element that is brought out and placed in the foreground. One does not exalt a person's good qualities by using caricature. It is used to represent a negative characteristic, especially social or psychological, such as overweight due to sloth or laziness, thievery, political corruption, ignorance, docility, or some other characteristic that needs to be rebuked. Moreover, caricature is a strong tool in the hands of an original and demanding writer; it can cut, tear, and hurt. It can be gentle, but it can also be vindictive, slicing and castrating, as when coming from V.S. Naipaul. Caricatures can be considered as overloaded representation (the English word 'caricature' derives from the Italian verb *caricare*, meaning 'to load'). It is "a representation, pictorial or descriptive, in which beauties are concealed and peculiarities or defects exaggerated so as to make the person or thing ridiculous, while a general likeness is retained" (*New Webster Encyclopedic Dictionary*).

It is important to note that caricatures can be classified into distinct types according to functions: social/political; personal; and aesthetic. Social/political caricature is the type mostly used by writers and novelists. Basically, it is a form that can be very vindictive and mocking, used for exposing negative aspects of personality, or some social and political situation. The second type is used for personal criticism. A characteristic or attribute is exaggerated in a comic fashion. This type can be dark, humorous and even retaliatory, but as with social/political caricature, it is critical of something or someone. The third type is the one utilised for aesthetic purposes, and can be looked at as a "half-caricature" because the vindictive and critical sense has not been totally wrought out. This type of caricature has an aesthetic function. It is used to improve on the author's style and form. It can add a light humour to passages, and can enhance the author's style. In Naipaul we can identify all three types of caricature. Other contemporary writers use caricature as a vehicle for criticism and comment. This is the case of Maryse Condé and Ngugi wa Thiong'o, whom I have included in this paper for comparative purposes.

Naipaul has worked and developed a knack for caricatures since his early Trinidadian novels. One critic implies the use of caricature by Naipaul, albeit not mentioning the word as such: "What distancing there is in the novel [*The Suffrage of Elvira*] is effected through the *comic exaggeration* and the elements of the *highly grotesque* and *absurd*" (my emphasis).[12] Others have used the term 'cartoon' or 'grotesque representation.' This brings us to something that is different from the caricature but is sometimes mistaken for it, i.e. the stereotype. A stereotype is always a false statement that can verge on bias and prejudice.

In his early fictional works about Trinidad, *Miguel Street* (1959) and *A House for Mr Biswas* (1961), Naipaul offers proliferating caricatures of places, persons and situations. He said that the anonymous Spanish picaresque novel, *Lazarillo de Tormes* (1554), was enormously influential on the writing of *Miguel Street* and on all his subsequent writings, especially on the "tone of that voice." He says:

> It is about a little poor boy growing up in Spain, in great imperial Spain, a very short book. But the *tone of that voice* was something that I loved [...] I found that it fitted my personality[13] (my emphasis).

This is very important because what really intrigued Naipaul in this picaresque novel was the use of the comical tone and, most of all, the caricatures. *Lazarillo* contains abundant caricatures that give it a sense of humour in the midst of severity and suffering. Another important factor, according to Derrick, is the influence of Dickens on Naipaul's work, especially *Miguel Street*.[14] This is significant because Dickens was himself influenced by the great Spanish picaresque writers of the Baroque period: Cervantes, Quevedo, Mateo Alemán and Vicente Espinel.

I have already made some comments about the continued presence of the comical in his most serious works. Naipaul masterfully combines comedy with the stark reality of suffering and hardship, a kind of comedy-horror, and follows through with a careful and original use of caricature. Comedy is everywhere in Naipaul's later works. He responds to Tejpal about the more grim, serious tone of his later novels after the three social comedies, and he insists that, even though there is tragedy and seriousness, there is also an underpinning of comedy.

> [...] the tone is not grim. It's full of comedy. The comedy is there, the comedy is less verbal, less farcical. I can read a page of my writing, any book, however dark you might think, and you'll laugh. I assure you that. It's full of jokes [...]. Without that, one couldn't have gone on. You can't give a dark, tragic view all the time. It must be supported by this deep underlying comedy.[15]

In his earlier Trinidadian text, *Miguel Street*, there is a delight in human comedy; in Derrick's words:

> The sheer buoyancy and comic exuberance of *Miguel Street*, the apparent casualness of its framework, reflect Naipaul's delight in the human comedy he creates. Repeatedly he draws attention not so much to the fact of failing in one sense or another as to the comic ironies and incongruities associated with it.[16]

Sometimes in Naipaul's works there is this urgency for style and form as opposed to idea or content: the caricature, the image, the situation, the satiric rhetoric. From these earlier works on, Naipaul has been a prolific writer of fiction and non-fiction using with art this critical tool of the caricature. But sometimes it leads to confusing situations and to misinterpretations by many critics. Some refer to him as a "racist," others as a "chauvinist" or "colonial lackey."[17] One gets the impression that Naipaul is gloating over the exaggerated representations that he uses, which go beyond humour and sometimes end up in a vindictive revenge of some kind. He does not spare children or old women; animals are caricatured (e.g. "thin village dogs"), and so too are plants (e.g. the water lilies with their "rubbery" vines growing wildly over the river and clogging the waterways). Europeans, Africans, Asians are treated in the same fashion by the hand of the master caricaturist. No one is spared. Clearly, racism is not the main issue in Naipaul's work, despite the generalisations of some.

Adewale Maja Pearce criticises Naipaul for his supposedly insidious statements against Africa and Black Africans, citing a passage from *In a Free State* that says the following: "The African opened the door himself. He filled the car with his smell [...] creating little turbulences of stink [...]."[18] This passage and other similar ones document, according to this critic, V.S. Naipaul's racial attitude. For the critic this passage identifies a stereotype of Black Africans; other critics will find in this passage a social caricature emanating from the narrative voice or speaker. Why does one critic view this as a stereotype while another views it as a caricature? These misunderstandings and apparent contradictions need to be discussed and analysed by Naipaul critics everywhere. It will not suffice to divide Naipaul scholarship into two opposing camps and reduce it to such simplicity. His art of fiction is much more complex; it brings into play authorial objectivity, multiple narrative viewpoints which are often not obvious, complex thematic strands, and heavy shades of tone.

A detailed reading of *A Bend in the River* identifies many passages in which caricatures are developed. In these passages one can identify all three types mentioned above. But mostly we have the social/political and the personal types working throughout his African texts. People from different ethnic groups are caricatured, such as Arabs, East Indians, Africans, even Europeans. Not only are humans caricatured, but also animals such as dogs, and plants too. Sometimes these representations are only half-caricatures, not truly formed ones. This is true, perhaps, of the hyacinths growing along the river, about which Cooke observes: "Assuming, after Heraclitus, that a river's flow represents the passage of time, the hyacinth-choked river is an image of cultural stagnation. The vain attempts of the villagers to remove the hyacinths show the futility of trying to bring this town into *history*."[19] The water hyacinths form an important part of the imagery of this new world landscape where there is stasis and stagnation, no future, no hope anywhere. Even the water hyacinths are slightly caricatured because Naipaul wants to impregnate the landscape with an aura, a meaning of temporal stagnation like the clogging of a water pipe with debris. Time has stopped and, perhaps, has "gone back in the primordial stew of the past" as Cooke comments (157).

Animals are also often represented in a grotesque manner. Since we are interested in human caricatures in Naipaul's fiction, we will briefly analyse some caricatures in which an animal or a thing is portrayed and then proceed to a fuller discussion of human caricatures. These are examples of aesthetic types of caricature which illustrate in order to add a certain zest to Naipaul's style and descriptions. Their function is mostly stylistic. When Salim goes out to the market he describes the animals that are sold for food as follows:

> Basins of grubs and caterpillars; baskets of trussed-up hens, squawking when they were lifted by one wing by the vendor or a prospective buyer; *dull-eyed* goats on the bare, scuffed ground, chewing at rubbish and even paper; damp-haired

> young monkeys, *full of misery*, tethered tightly around their narrow waists and nibbling at peanuts and banana skin and mango skin, but nibbling *without relish*, as though *they knew that they themselves were soon to be eaten*[20] (my emphasis).

The words and phrases highlighted give human qualities to animals and are part of the scheme of caricature development. They offer the reader a kind of grim portrayal of what awaits these store animals. Naipaul's caricatures are extremely humorous, but at the same time, very serious, angry statements about his subjects. Campbell uses the term "refinement" to explain Naipaul's treatment of his own rage in his fiction.[21]

In another passage Naipaul describes the growth of the town's population. It is a question of picking up the garbage, and if there is money to pay the military, then certainly there should also be money to fix up the town and pick up the garbage. His use, therefore, of caricature is well taken; it has a social-critical function:

> The growth of the population could be gauged by the growth of the rubbish heaps in the cités. They didn't burn their rubbish in oil drums, as we did; they just threw it out on the broken streets—that sifted, ashy African rubbish. Those mounds of rubbish, though constantly flattened by rain, grew month by month into increasingly solid little hills, and the hills literally became as high as the box-like concrete houses of the cités (*ABR* 87).

In another passage a dog is represented through caricature:

> And then a large Doberman came bounding out at me. The man with the fork said, Don't worry. He'll miss you. He can't see very well. A foreigner's dog. He gave it to me when he went away. It was as he said. The Doberman *missed me by about a foot*, ran on a little way, stopped, raced back, and then was all over me, wagging his docked tail, beside himself with joy at my foreigner's smell,

> *momentarily mistaking me for somebody else* (*ABR* 260) (my emphasis).

In this last passage the representation is only a half-caricature—but an interesting one, for the dog wags its tail thanks to Salim's foreign smell. Also, the dog is easily confused or fooled; it lacks any clear-cut vision of the situation. Animals are, thus, also treated in terms of cynicism and tragedy. This dog is a "colonial" dog; he is a subject of the colonist, wagging his tail in obedience, careful always to please his "master." Above all, he "can't see very well." The dog is certainly a mocking representation of the colonized. There are also many passages in which landscape is caricatured.[22] Even so, the bulk of Naipaul's criticism is directed towards individuals who represent some type of unethical stance, some neo-colonial situation—or a person who just has plain bad blood.

Naipaul is heavily influenced by Joseph Conrad's particular way of describing things and people, especially in *Heart of Darkness.* This is especially so in the case of Conrad's use of stark, naked and morbid caricatures. *Heart of Darkness* contains some memorable representations that can be classified as social-political. Conrad's world is not humorous, but serious, sombre, full of fear, ominous. His caricatures are not comical; there is no mocking or ridiculing, but there is a grave critical sense. The images are deadly and horrible, ghastly and inferno-like. They communicate a serious tone of the terrible, the dark depths that human beings can plunge into; but they are true caricatures because they exaggerate some characteristic or attribute to make it stand out. This creates a protrusion, a kind of engraving of the description which serve as blunt political criticism.

> Black shapes crouched, lay, sat between the trees, leaning against the trunks, clinging to the earth, half coming out, half effaced within the dim light, in all the attitudes of pain, abandonment, and despair [...]. These moribund shapes were free as air—and nearly as thin [...].[23]

There is nothing humorous or comic in this description. This is what is left of human beings after colonialism. Here we can see how Conrad has been mistaken or misunderstood. He is not mocking or laughing at Africans, not being a racist, but pitying them in their condition, to say the least. A few lines earlier, Marlow makes the following statement: "They were not enemies, they were not criminals, they were nothing earthly now—nothing but black shadows of disease and starvation [...] Brought from all the recesses of the coast in all the legality of time contracts [...]" (*HD* 17). Conrad is certainly critical of the whole colonial enterprise and what it has done to the African people. The caricatures transform the subjects into deformed and grotesque things, but this is part of the style in the making of caricatures. They are ugly and horrible exaggerations of real life. In other passages he depicts the African to make a grim statement of what the colonial enterprise did to human beings:

> While I stood horror-struck, one of these creatures rose to his hands and knees, and went off on all fours towards the river to drink. He lapped out of his hand, then sat up in the sunlight, crossing his shins in front of him, and after a time let his woolly head fall on his breastbone (*HD* 18).

These are examples of caricatures that lack humour and comedy because they are representations of human tragedy and suffering. It is odd and illogical how some critics can claim that racism is portrayed in these passages. On the contrary, one can appreciate the deep humanity of Joseph Conrad in the way he rebukes and depicts human suffering. The representations here have the important function of criticizing the whole colonial enterprise in Africa. I think Conrad's use of some words has been totally misinterpreted and misjudged by many. In the following passage the word 'nigger' should be re-interpreted by taking into account the complete passage that serves as a critical statement by Conrad of the colonial situation:

> A nigger was being beaten near by. They said he had caused the fire in some way; be that as it may, he was screeching most horribly. I saw him, later, for several days, sitting in a

> bit of shade looking very sick and trying to recover himself: afterwards he arose and went out—and the wilderness without a sound took him into its bosom again (*HD* 24).

Certainly, this is a caricature, but very grim and horrible; the African does not scream out in pain, but screeches. There is nothing funny here; it is an intentional depiction by Conrad of human suffering. The grim sense of Conrad is always present in Naipaul's writing, and the use of caricature has been very instrumental. There is an affinity between Conrad and Naipaul, not only in subject- matter, but also in style, the use of imagery and the serious, sombre tone.

Maryse Condé, in *Heremakhonon*, uses irony, sarcasm and mockery in Veronica's interior monologue and stream of consciousness. But the author also uses caricatures, in a limited sense, to communicate these feelings and moods. In *Heremakhonon* she uses caricatures that are very similar in tone and sense to Naipaul's. They are strong, and at times even vindictive in nature. These caricatures serve as social criticism as the passages below illustrates:

> Instead of a *balding, wheezing white with a limp prick*, I'd have myself a rich young mulatto with a *permanent hard on.* Aunt Paula came to Paris. She was wealthy. Jean-Michel and I took her out. She was wearing an enormous *necklace and earrings the size of avocados.* Real gold![24] (my emphasis).

In another passage a personal type of criticism with a hint of the social is employed:

> The next morning he's still there. With a cup of coffee instead of a glass of whiskey. At his side, Marilisse, real name Adama. She *chews on her toothpick* and *emits a strong odour* (Blacks stink; everyone knows that.) (*HER* 17) (my emphasis).

Here Condé not only caricatures white people, but also Africans. Take for example the following caricature representing her fellow African, Ramatoulaye:

> Just as I'm wondering which way to go, with the sun battering me on the head, a Mercedes draws up level with me. Inside, a woman draped *in a gold lamé boubou*, a Carita wig, *chewing a 10-inch long stick* [...] (*HER* 69) (my emphasis).

Veronica, herself an African-Caribbean, is making fun of a fellow African; it is mainly the artificiality and mimicry of the subject which Veronica despises. She is not interested in hiding the faults, weaknesses and mimicry of her fellow Africans, but is very critical of mimicry. Agossou, Ibrahim's servant, is represented as: "already at work with a green plastic hose in his hand. He gives me a *toothless smile*" (*HER* 72). And Abdoulaye, Ibrahim's butler, is described as "rushing" up to meet Veronica. She finds this strange: a black man having black servants, almost slaves. For Veronica this is a contradiction; it is difficult to digest the customs, the ideas, the priorities of this new native African environment filled with violence and corruption:

> I suppose the master is having his siesta like the rest of the town. They sleep everywhere at this time. The town is inhabited by fetus—cluttering the market, a stinking womb, blocking Independence Square, under the big trees, burdening the wharves [...] (*HER* 92).

The image of the African Baké is extremely grotesque:

> A waiter brings us a bottle of champagne wrapped in a none too clean rag in an ice bucket and points to a kind of mastodon, the type of man I can't stand, with his head as polished as a mirror and bright, staring eyes, dressed in a brown gandourah and patent leather shoes (*HER* 107).

The image is that of a mobster sort of fellow with certain characteristics standing out. Veronica describes this fellow: "Baké and his thick lips." These are excellent personal caricatures. Condé is not manifesting racism but her disgust. Conrad has anti-colonial sentiments, and Naipaul despises the mimicry of power elites in Africa, who are only interested in their own welfare and their neo-colonial sponsors. Veronica, Condé's protagonist, suffers from the paradoxes and contradictions of her modern-day Africa, which is also corrupt and incongruous.

Naipaul develops caricatures for everyone, regardless of race, colour, creed, nationality, or ethnic group. Each of these caricatures has a specific message, a critical Naipaulian comment, and they should be analysed in these terms. In his early African novel, *In a Free State*, which consists of three interesting narratives, related thematically to the isolated and alienated individual in a foreign country, Naipaul brilliantly uses caricature to portray people's attitudes and behaviour. In "One out of Many," Santosh, the principal character, an Indian servant brought to Washington, D.C. by his master, meets a "hubshi" (Afro-American) woman and describes her as follows:

> A few days later I had my adventure. The hubshi woman came in, moving among my employer's ornaments *like a bull.* I was greatly provoked. The smell was too much; so was the *sight of her armpits.* I fell. She dragged me down on the couch, on the saffron spread which was one of my employer's nicest pieces of Punjabi folk-weaving. I saw the moment, helplessly, as one of dishonour. I saw her as Kali, goddess of death and destruction, *coal-black, with a red tongue and white eyeballs and many powerful arms.* I expected her to be wild and fierce; but she added insult to injury by being very playful, as though, because I was small and strange, the act was not real. She laughed all the time [...][25] (my emphasis).

Some critics may indict Naipaul for his representation of Blacks, but the importance of this caricature is that Santosh is a foreigner, lacking the appropriate cultural knowledge that can be translated into correct behaviour. He is a stranger, ignorant of the customs and ideas of people in the ghetto in Washington, D.C. He can only interpret reality through his own set of cultural paradigms, foreign images and sensations overpower him. Santosh, the narrator, uses a very native Indian viewpoint.

Naipaul uses cultural code-switching in a very creative manner. In an interview Naipaul once said: "Since I went to India I've become interested in the way different cultures have different ways of seeing."[26] Modern society consists of many cultural layers, one on top of another, sometimes creating conflicts and tensions, and this is utilised in his fiction.

In his novels, cultural reference points are always shifting, and for a European, American, or even African readership there might be some confusion, some misinterpretation of narrative perspective. Santosh is striving to understand his predicament, coming to terms with his new foreign ambience. Phillip Langran says that Naipaul's diversity of cultural knowledge has placed him, or perhaps, transformed him into a kind of universal writer, one who can go in and out, and understand, different cultural contexts: "Naipaul paves the way for an even more controlled and dispassionate body of work which increasingly emphasizes placelessness and cultural disorder as a universal, rather than purely West Indian condition."[27] And so it is with Salim, the narrator of *A Bend in the River*. In this novel, Naipaul is very careful in the use of the narrative voice. Even though the narrator is Salim, there are multiple narrative viewpoints coming from Salim; he is not alone. One can also hear other narrators, such as Indar, Raymond and Nazrudim. They are also narrating their personal philosophies, ideas, insights, and prejudices.

In Salim's voice one can hear Naipaul's personal views; but also one can hear other viewpoints: ideas that are gathered by the author from personal experiences, from his visits and tours, from his friends, even his enemies. It is not only Naipaul talking through Salim, but others too; there are dozens of voices rumbling through the narrative voice, each of these expounding viewpoints, ideas, prejudices, false arguments, truths. The Naipaulian universe, viewed correctly, is not a simple phenomenon that can be interpreted using a simple arithmetic formula; it is highly complex and convoluted. It is a juxtaposition of various perspectives and viewpoints using the narrative voice along with development of characters, exposing the neo-colonial mind, and using the right amount of satire, sarcasm, irony and contradiction.

Let us identify a few passages in *A Bend in the River* in which caricatures are developed for representing individuals. No one is spared; everyone is caricatured: the Arab, the Indian, the African, the Belgian, the insane and mentally incompetent, the common man. When Salim arrives in the town around the bend, he meets a few people, mostly Asian or Indian. An Indian couple he meets is described in a grotesque original representation.

> There was a couple from India. They lived in a small flat that smelled of asafoetida and was decorated with paper flowers and brightly coloured religious prints [...]. They were a hospitable couple and they made a point of offering hospitality to frightened or stranded foreigners [...]. Their food was too liquid and peppery for me, and *I didn't like the way the man ate.* He bent his *head low over his food,* keeping his nose an inch or two away from his plate and he ate noisily, *slapping his lips together.* While he ate like this his wife fanned him, never taking her eyes off his plate, fanning with her right hand, resting her chin on the palm of her left hand (*ABR* 28) (my emphasis).

This caricature has a humorous and comic function. We can at least say that the gentleman did not have table manners. Or we may say that the image communicates degradation of some sort. But it might be interpreted as cruel. Our modern world has conditioned itself and sees comedy in horror and suffering. Death and torture are seen nowadays as comical events or jokes. At the end of the passage Naipaul has the narrator say: "Still, I went there twice a week more for the sake of having somewhere to go than for the food" (*ABR* 28). The function of the caricature is stylistic and formal because it balances the whole description.

Ferdinand, the young African student from the bush, is described as follows:

> I smiled at Ferdinand and he smiled at me, pulling back the corners of his mouth. The smile made me notice the neatness of his mouth and the sharp-cut quality of the rest of his features. In his face I felt I could see the starting point of certain kinds of African masks, in which features were simplified and strengthened; and, with memories of those masks, I thought I saw a special distinction in his features (*ABR* 37).

Here we have a comment on the simple style and carvings of African art at the time. A vagueness is communicated by Salim, as if to portray a kind of tabula rasa in which the Big Man can have the opportunity of impressing Ferdinand with suitable new African qualities. In another section, Salim looks at Ferdinand with a fear and dread, because he can see the future transformation of this youth into a military or government man, faithfully and blindly following the orders of the Big Man: "He was frightening, and the thought came to me. This is how he will look when he sees his victim's blood, when he watches his enemy being killed. And climbing on that thought was another: 'This is the rage that flattened the town'" (*ABR* 59).

The town is filled with petty thieves: "The town, run down as it was, crawled with thieves, and they seemed able to *wriggle through any little opening*" (*ABR* 41) (my emphasis). This is an example of a very sharp caricature whose function is more stylistic but, also, reinforcing idea. These caricatures are like intentional pauses in the narrative in order to give the reader a space for rest. This is true of Naipaul's representation when Salim is waiting at the airport for his flight back to the town from his London trip. In this caricature an African is portrayed in a primitive manner, combining the old Africa with the new in a humorous mixture:

> [...] a barefooted man turned up wearing a fireman's helmet with the transparent plastic visor pulled down. He was an

> old man with a shrunken face; his brown shorts and grey check shirt were ragged and soaked through. I thought: He's found a ready-made dancing mask. He went from table to table, checking the beer bottles. When he decided that a bottle was worth emptying he raised the visor of his mask and drank [...]. Then we went out to the wet field to board it. I saw the man with the fireman's helmet—and a companion, also helmeted—standing unsteadily beside the gangway. *He was, after all, a fireman* (*ABR* 253) (my emphasis).

This person was not someone coming out of the bush and serving as a garbage collector; he was a genuine fireman! The author tried to represent the illogical and irrational mixing of the two Africa with this caricature. Naipaul has a strange sense of humour, sometimes twisted, but always very original. In all the passages mentioned above one can appreciate the literary inheritance of the picaresque novel in Naipaul's work. In fact, the whole framework of the picaresque, the use of caricature, the irony and sarcasm, the realistic details, are part of the literary inheritance of the Renaissance. One can take the influence back to the Archpriest of Hita, Boccaccio and Cervantes, and bring it right up to Dickens' use of caricature in *Oliver Twist* and *David Copperfield*. Some of these sources, along with *El Lazarrillo* have been influential in Naipaul's work.

While in London, Nazruddin tells Salim about his business projects and some of his failures. He informs Salim about the eventual bush enveloping Europe and America: "All over the world money is in flight. People have scraped the world clean, as clean as an African can scrape his yard, and now they want to run from the dreadful places where they've made their money and find some nice safe country" (*ABR* 234). Naipaul puts a sharp and cutting caricature of Arabs into Nazruddin's mouth:

> The little flat was full of poor Arabs in undershirts and horribly coloured pants. There was bedding all over the floor. The girl wasn't with them. They had sent her away,

> or she had left. For two months, while I had been paying twenty per cent interest and other charges, I had been giving free shelter to a whole *tentful* of poor Arabs. They are a strange people racially. One of them had bright red hair. What were they doing in London? (*ABR* 238)
>
> Sometimes I saw little groups of poor Arabs in dingy clothes squatting on the grass in the park or on the pavements of the streets nearby (*ABR* 233).

In these two passages Arabs are caricatured not because they are poor and "dirty," but because they represent the *oddity* of the neo-colonial situation, a kind of paradox and absurdity in the modern world, where contradictions live side by side in a confused and incongruous manner.

An African officer in the town is depicted in these terms: "sweating under the arms in his over-starched uniform, and he was writing very slowly in a ledger, shaping one letter at a time, apparently entering details from the blotched finger print sheets" (*ABR* 209). The officer is probably illiterate, yet he has the power and authority to carry a revolver and shoot someone he dislikes—and, of course, discipline *avant tout.*

Naipaul, no doubt, gloated over and totally enjoyed his depiction of the bureaucratic Indian government worker in London. He is fat, gross and totally lost in his caste philosophy. Naipaul's anger is felt in this passage. But he "refines" his rage by utilizing appropriate images. Here we also have two opposing worldviews trying to coalesce or mingle: the traditional Indian worldview with the European vision. Contradiction will, no doubt, appear when something is forced into a pre-existing mould from either side:

> His shiny cheeks were swollen with fat and his lips appeared to pout. I sat down on a chair placed some distance away from his desk. He didn't look up at me and he didn't speak. And I didn't speak; I let him open his letters. Not an hour's exercise had he taken in his life, this devout man of

> the South. He reeked of caste and temple, and I was sure that below that black suit he wore all kinds of amulets (*ABR* 149).

It is the mimicry of trying to talk, act, behave and be like someone from another culture, another viewpoint, another place and time. For Naipaul it is artificial and plastic; it's like producing an 'instant' civilization or society overnight. Something that has taken a millennium to construct can be now reproduced in a few weeks: modern Africa, India, Asia, Latin America. Some are interested sincerely in having their countries develop socially, economically and ideologically; but others are interested in playing a game, a little corrupt game of how much they can get out of a country or a situation. African military men and police are depicted sharply: "[they] wore gold as much as possible—gold-rimmed glasses, gold rings, gold pen-and-pencils sets, gold watches with solid gold wristlets. Among ourselves we scoffed at the vulgarity and pathos of that African lust for gold [...]" (*ABR* 119). Naipaul is not saying this in a categorical sense; he is not saying that all African military men and police are this way. It is not the Africans per se who are criticised, but individuals who are mimics and are corrupt. In another section the author writes about some other uniformed military Africans:

> I thought these new officers stood for a new, constructive pride. But they were simpler. The flag and the President's portrait were only like their fetishes, the sources of their authority. They didn't see, these young men, that there was anything to build in their country. As far as they were concerned, it was all there already. They had only to take. They believed that, by being what they were, they had earned the right to take; and the higher the officer, *the greater the crookedness*—if that word had any meaning [...] With their guns and jeeps, these men were poachers of ivory and thieves of gold [...] (*ABR* 91) (my emphasis).

Even the opposing camp of the rebels is represented mockingly. They have a genuine African rage in their blood. Everything that smacks of Europe and America must be done away with, must be obliterated. Mobutu's back-to-Africa campaign and its roots are well remembered. But there is a slightly more rude and primitive sense by the rebels, according to Salim: "The rage of the rebels was like a rage *against metal, machinery, wires,* everything that was not of the forest and Africa" (*ABR* 81) (my emphasis). This remark is quite astounding; it might be interpreted as a description of compulsive-obsessive behaviour. We are on the verge of insanity; in fact, *A Bend* can be said to be a novel, like Conrad's *Heart of Darkness,* about impending insanity, compulsive-obsessive behaviour on a grand national scale.

There is a comical sense in the following caricature representing an African hotel worker, a kind of manager. It is an example of a simple caricature used for style, but extremely comical with a streak of cynicism. I include it as a final example of Naipaul's use of caricature in *ABR*: "[...] the big-bellied African (from down river somewhere) who normally stood behind the reception desk cleaning his teeth with a toothpick and being rude to everybody, but was now standing by the suitcases and trying to look busy and serious" (*ABR* 73). Some readers would apparently be struck dumbfounded at such an image because the caricature does not deal with a German or British subject, nor does it deal with an American. Our society nowadays is so racially conscious and sensitive that any word or suggestion, racial or ethnically oriented, will pour out protests, indignations and insults. For many critics, a writer must not write what he feels or thinks, but what is politically correct, or what is committed. Naipaul detests such arguments and views; they contradict the whole notion of what literature should strive for, whether social or aesthetic.

By contrast with Naipaul's, Conrad's and Condé's use of caricature with intensity, emotion and deep irony, satire and sarcasm, Ngugi's caricatures in *The Devil on the Cross* are not that well developed.[28] They lack the sufficient punch of sarcasm, vindictiveness and mockery that is so characteristic of Naipaul's excellent caricatures. Ngugi's caricatures are more neutral than critical, even though the author is trying to express political censure through his use of caricatures:

> On another day an American tourist hired this car. This American was really old. His face was full of deep valleys. And on the other parts of his body, the folds of the skin lay in rolling layers. But he had with him an African girl, [...] Foam dribbled out of the sides of his mouth, and he groaned as if the real deed were on (*DEV* 71).

In this passage, Mwaura, the taxi owner, is describing an incident that occurred to him. But the caricature portrayed doesn't have that critical sense; it does not include that emotional sarcastic punch that Naipaul utilises. Ngugi's representation is a bland statement, lacking the mocking tone which is so important in caricature portrayals. In another passage this can also be seen:

> Barmaids moved from table to table, taking orders for drinks. They were all dressed in catsuits of black wool. The suits were form-fitting: they clung to the contours of the girls' bodies so closely that a distant onlooker might have thought that the girls were naked. On the girls' bottoms were fixed small white patches shaped like rabbit's tails. On their breasts were pinned two plastic fruits. Each girl also wore a band around her head on which was written in English: I love you. The girls looked like apparitions from another world (*DEV* 92).

Here we have the author trying to caricature the barmaids but he is having difficulty in doing this. There is no irony or mockery anywhere; caricatures are known for at least an ironic sense. This is one of the weakest caricatures in *Devil on the Cross*. It is just a blunt critical statement with no artistic and literary embellishment whatsoever. One caricature that does have a humorous sarcastic sense is the portrait of Gitutu wa Gataanguru:

> Gitutu had a belly that protruded so far that it would have

> touched the ground had it not been supported by the braces that held up his trousers. It seemed as if his belly had absorbed all his limbs and all the other organs of his body. Gitutu had no neck—at least, his neck was not visible. His arms and legs were short stumps. His head had shrunk to the size of a fist.[29]

Here Ngugi uses social caricature, but he fails to give enough force to his representation; it lacks vindictiveness and mockery. Nevertheless, this caricature is one of the author's best. Another caricature that is interesting and comical is the representation of Kihaahu wa Gatheeca:

> Kihaahu was a tall, slim fellow: he had long legs, long arms, long finger, a long neck and a long mouth. His mouth was shaped like the beak of the kingstock: long, thin and sharp. His chin, his face, his head formed a cone. Everything about him indicated leanness and sharp cunning [...].
>
> That day, Kihaahu was dressed in black-and-grey striped trousers, a black tail coat, a white shirt and a black tie. Standing [...], he looked like a 6-foot praying mantis or mosquito (*DEV* 108).

In this passage Ngugi is exerting himself in portraying something that can be mocked and laughed at. He succeeds to an extent, but the writing is not emotionally charged. It lacks that Naipaulian punch—the vindictiveness, the mocking insult, the slap in the mouth.[30]

Let us compare and take, for example, one of Naipaul's caricatures that is short and to the point, but has a solid punch. It focuses on the Islamic world and Ayatollah Khalkhali. This is the way Naipaul sees a corrupt megalomania that has power in its hand to kill and destroy anything or anyone who disagrees "[...] choking with laughter, showing me his gums, his tongue, his gullet."[31] Naipaul has created a very complex caricature functioning as a social/political criticism, and consisting of an amalgam of irony, satire and mockery—all squeezed into just one simple, but extremely crafted line.

V.S. Naipaul has been awarded prizes and insults from both sides. He has been acclaimed as a leading novelist since the 1960s, and at the same time has been labelled a "colonial lackey," "neo-colonial spokesman," "racist," and "assimilationist." It seems that there are more insults than prizes. It is certain that, although critics have liberally interpreted his message to be noble-ignoble, truthful-false, racist-prejudiced and moral-ethical, at the same time, Naipaul is, beyond doubt, a great master of fiction and literary device, a craftsman of style and imagery. His art is one of reducing complexities to simple images; of creating original descriptions that are pregnant with suggestive possibilities. The author is constantly trying to understand the human condition. It is certain that Naipaul has human and ethical qualities; he is not a monster. He is worried at what man may be capable of doing, in man's capacity for lying and self-deception. Naipual must be placed in the category of writers who are ethical and worried about human rights. But like Joseph Conrad, he has been misunderstood and misinterpreted.

In this paper we have endeavoured to present not a political discussion or controversy, but an exploration and study of one interesting facet of Naipaul's fiction, i.e. his imaginative and creative use of caricature and how it is utilised as a socio-critical tool. Throughout his work, from his early Trinidadian novels to his latest African, Indian and Asian adventures, the use of caricature has been one of Naipaul's formidable signatures. The sense of humour has not been lost; it is still prevalent in both his fiction and non-fiction, even in the midst of terror and torture. Caricature can be funny and humorous, but at the same time, it can fulfil the function of social and ideological criticism. It is one of the ways in which a true artist can portray and refine his "rage," and emit his opinion in a world of turmoil. Naipaul has faithfully achieved this in his fiction. He is out to unveil and unmask these terrors and rags. Elaine Campbell writes:

Naipaul brings examination and re-examination of today's

> facile usage of the terms 'slave' and 'free' and he refuses to permit persecution to be muffled and washed away in the *rhetoric of revolution.* His cause may not be popular, but as gadfly to the Third World, Naipaul serves an invaluable function"[32] (my emphasis).

Naipaul is not merely content to describe objectively all the pitfalls and injustices that occur under neo/postcolonial regimes: he also uses his subjective voice to criticise them sharply and with force.

Christopher Wise writes: "Hence, Naipaul does not so much offer us the unmediated observations, of an irresponsible free-agent as he presents us with the [...] determined insights or even 'truths' of a deeply disenfranchised subject of the Third World in the era of multinational capitalism—which is to say, neocolonialism."[33] Naipaul, like Conrad, has been mistaken by many avid young critics who are embittered and angry at the residue of colonialism. But they fail to realise that Naipaul has been, precisely, hacking at this neo-colonialism for well over 45 years. As Scott Winokur puts it in an interview with Naipaul:

> The Third World he has written about for the last four decades is—in his dark, unblinking eyes—a festering sore, a realm of instinct and delusion controlled by corrupt leaders who prefer to lay blame for current misfortunes on *accidents of history and long-gone colonizers,* rather than to look *inward* and exercise what Naipaul calls 'the gift of self-criticism'"[34] (my emphasis).

But only time will tell what the neo-colonial regimes and the power elites in these nations will do; and then, people will re-read and re-interpret Naipaul, but in a new and different light.

Notes

1. V.S. Naipaul, *A Bend in the River* (New York: Vintage Press, 1980) 100 (subsequently *ABR*).
2. Stephen Schiff, "The Ultimate Exile," *The New Yorker* 23 May 1994: 61; cited in Jussawalla.

3. A.C. Derrick, "Naipaul's Technique as a Novelist," *The Journal of Commonwealth Literature* 7 (1969): 32.
4. Tarun J. Tejpal, "V.S. Naipaul's *Way in the World,*" <www.randomhouse.com/atrandom/vsnaipaul, 5.>
5. V.S. Naipaul, *The Return of Eva Peron* (London: Andre Deutsch, 1980) 199; subsequent citations *REP*.
6. Published in *The New York Review of Books*; subsequently compiled with the "Killings" and the article on Eva Peron in: *The Return of Eva Peron*.
7. Prescott wrote an article about Naipaul's sources for *A Bend* which includes a discussion of Joseph Conrad; also, Campbell's article deals with the novel's sources. See also: Linda Prescott, "Past and Present Darkness: Sources for V.S. Naipaul's *A Bend in the River,*" *Modern Fiction Studies* 30.3 (1984): 547-59; Elaine Campbell, "A Refinement of Rage: V.S. Naipaul's *A Bend in the River,*" *World Literature Written in English* 18 (1979): 394-406.
8. In a recently published article, I discuss the major techniques that Naipaul uses in his travel narratives and connect these with his fictional elements: "V.S. Naipaul's Vulcanization of Travel and Fiction Paradigms," *The Atlantic Literary Review* 2.3 (July-Sept. 2001): 143-73.
9. Tejpal 19.
10. On the relationship between *Heart of Darkness* and *A Bend in the River*, see: Peter Nazareth, "Out of Darkness: Conrad and other Third World Writers," *Conradiana: A Journal of Joseph Conrad* 14.3 (1982): 173-87; and Rudy Duyck, "V.S. Naipaul's *Heart of Darkness,*" *ACLALS Bulletin* 7.4 (1986): 86-94.
11. Naipaul, *REP* 219.
12. Derrick 36.
13. Tejpal 7.
14. Derrick 33.
15. Tejpal 11.
16. Derrick 34.
17. Berger offers no future for Naipaul and indicts him: "It is therefore unlikely that criticism—humanistic or poststructuralist—can recuperate Naipaul's work." Roger A. Berger, "Writing Without a Future: Colonial Nostalgia in V.S. Naipaul's *A Bend in the River,*" *Essays in Literature* 22.1 (1995) 153.
18. Quoted in Adewale Maja Pearce, "The Naipauls on Africa: an African View," *The Journal of Commonwealth Literature* 20.1 (1985): 111.

19. John Cooke, "A Vision of the Land: V.S. Naipaul's Later Novels," *Journal of Caribbean Studies* 1 (1980): 158.
20. Naipaul, *ABR* 159.
21. Campbell 396.
22. For a discussion of Naipaulian landscape, see Cooke.
23. Joseph Conrad, *Heart of Darkness* (New York: W. W. Norton, 1971) 17; subsequent citation in text *HD*.
24. Maryse Condé, *Heremakhonon* (London: Lynne Rienner, 2000) 9 [English translation]; subsequent citation in text as *HER*.
25. V.S. Naipaul, *In a Free State* (New York: Penguin Books, 1981) 38.
26. Ian Hamilton, "Without a Place: V.S. Naipaul Interviewed," *Savacou* 9-10 (1974): 125.
27. Phillip Langran, "V.S. Naipaul: A Question of Detachment," *The Journal of Commonwealth Literature* 25.1 (1990): 134.
28. Ngugi wa Thiong'o, *Devil on the Cross* (Oxford: Heinemann, 1987) 59. Subsequent citations in text as *DEV*.
29. Ngugi 99; Gitutu is portrayed in another caricature (108): "By the time Gitutu wa Gataanguru had finished his testimony, he was panting with fatigue. Drops of his sweat fell to the floor, His protruding belly was trembling as if it wanted to break loose and fall to the ground."
30. See also the caricature of Nditika wa Nguunji (176); it has similar traits to the above, but lacks that mocking tone and the vindictiveness that adds and transforms the punch into a knockout punch.
31. V.S. Naipaul, *Among the Believers: an Islamic Journey* (New York: Vintage, 1982) 55.
32. Campbell 402.
33. Wise 61.
34. Scott Winokur, "The Unsparing Vision of V.S. Naipaul," quoted in Feroza Jussawalla, ed., *Conversations with V.S. Naipaul* (Jackson: UP of Mississippi, 1997) 116.

Works Cited

Berger, Roger A. "Writing Without a Future: Colonial Nostalgia in V.S. Naipaul's *A Bend in the River*." *Essays in Literature* 22.1 (1995): 144-56.

Blakemore, Steven. "'An Africa of Words': V.S. Naipaul's *A Bend in the River*." *South Carolina Review* 18.1 (1985): 15-23.

Boxill, Anthony. *V.S. Naipaul's Fiction: In Quest of the Enemy*. Fredericton, Canada: York, 1983.

Campbell, Elaine. "A Refinement of Rage: V.S. Naipaul's *A Bend in the River*." *World Literature Written in English* 18 (1979): 394-406.

Cooke, John. "A Vision of the Land: V.S. Naipaul's Later Novels." *Journal of Caribbean Studies* 1 (1980): 140-61.

Day, Frank. "Naipaul's Vision of Wounded Civilizations." *South Carolina Review* 18.1 (1985): 10-14.

Derrick, A.C. "Naipaul's Technique as a Novelist." *The Journal of Commonwealth Literature* 7 (1969): 32-44.

Duyck, Rudy. "V.S. Naipaul and John Donne: the Morning After." *The Journal of Commonwealth Literature* 24.1 (1989): 155-62.

——. "V.S. Naipaul's Heart of Darkness." *ACLALS Bulletin* 7.4 (1986): 86-94.

Fersch, Annabelle F. "V.S. Naipaul's *A Bend in the River* and the Art of Re-Reading." *Commonwealth Novel in English* 5.2 (1992): 1-8.

Griffith, Glyne A. "Travel Narrative As Cultural Critique: V.S. Naipaul's Travelling Theory." *The Journal of Commonwealth Literature* 29.2 (1993): 87-92.

Guinness, Gerald. "Rev. of *London Calling: V.S. Naipaul, Postcolonial Mandarin*, by Rob Nixon." *Revista/Review Interamericana* (1993).

Hamilton, Ian. "Without a Place: V.S. Naipaul Interviewed." *Savacou* 9-10 (1974): 120-26.

Howe, Irving. "A Dark Vision: *A Bend in the River*." *New York Times Book Review* 13 May 1979: 1-2.

Hyland, Peter. *Discharging the Canon: Cross-Cultural Readings in Literature*. Singapore: Singapore UP, 1986.

Jama, Virginia. "The Image of the African Leader in Recent Western Fiction." *Horn of Africa* 3.1 (1980): 43-45.

Jussawalla, Feroza, ed. *Conversations with V.S. Naipaul*. Jackson, MS: UP of Mississippi, 1997.

Langran, Phillip. "V.S. Naipaul: A Question of Detachment." *The Journal of Commonwealth Literature* 25.1 (1990): 132-41.

Lavin, Marjorie Woods, and Fredric Agatstein. "Personal Identity and the Imagery of Place: Psychological Issues & Literary Themes." *Journal of Mental Imagery* 8.3 (1984): 51-66.

Maja Pearce, Adewale. "The Naipauls on Africa: an African View." *The Journal of Commonwealth Literature* 20.1 (1985): 111-17.

Michener, Charles. "The Dark Visions of V.S. Naipaul." *Newsweek* 16 Nov. 1981: 104-15.

Nazareth, Peter. "Out of Darkness: Conrad and Other Third World Writers." *Conradiana: A Journal of Joseph Conrad* 14.3 (1982): 173-87.

Prescott, Lynda. "Past and Present Darkness: Sources for V.S. Naipaul's *A Bend in the River*." *Modern Fiction Studies* 30.3 (1984): 547-59.

Pyne Timothy, Helen. "V.S. Naipaul and Politics: His View of Third-World Societies in Africa and the Caribbean." *CLA Journal* 28.3 (1985): 247-62.

_____. "Women and Sexuality in the Later Novels of V.S. Naipaul." *World Literature Written in English* 25.2 (1985): 298-306.

Singh, H. B. "V.S. Naipaul: A Spokesman for New-Colonialism." *Literature and Ideology* 2 (1969): 71-85.

Smyer, Richard. "Naipaul's *A Bend in the River*: Fiction and the Post-Colonial Tropics." *Literary Half-Yearly* 23.2 (1982): 59-68.

Tejpal, Tarun J. "V.S. Naipaul's *Way in the World*." Random House Web Page. URL: <www.randomhouse.com/atrandom/vsnaipaul>.

Wise, Christopher. "The Garden Trampled; or, The Liquidation of African Culture in V.S. Naipaul's *A Bend in the River*." *College Literature* 23.3 (1996): 58-72.

9

Young Monkey, New Tricks: Foreman's Apprenticeship in V.S. Naipaul's *The Suffrage of Elvira*

PASCAL P. BUMA

Published in 1958, *The Suffrage of Elvira* stands out as a satiric chronicle of the burgeoning democratic process in Elvira, a place small enough for people to know each other and where the potential voting pool numbers in the thousands, and where the top dogs, capable of influencing the outcome of politics are household names, known beyond mere acquaintance. Within this atmosphere that is bowing to the winds of change, there is Foreman Baksh, a young lad, who has come of age, and while he is not the central figure of the novel, there is enough focus on him to cause one to wonder if V.S. Naipaul intended to write a *Bildungsroman*, or whether the apparent maturation of Foam in the novel is simply incidental, intended to provide a vignette of two successive generations of the community of Elvira at the midpoint of the twentieth century. Critics interested in the question of taxonomy have, for obvious reasons, focused more on the social and political satire, considering the novel as a metaphor for Naipaul's mockery of the political transformation of Trinidad and Tobago. However, others have outrightly classified the novel as a *Bildungsroman*, the novel of growth, maturation, education and identity, in which the protagonist, after years of apprenticeship, finds a place within the social structure of his community and becomes a contributing member even though he might have rebelled against it and even run away from it at some point in his life. In her seminal book, *Ten Is the Age of Darkness: The Black Bildungsroman,* Geta LeSeur lists *The Suffrage of Elvira* as a *Bildungsroman* in the appendix. This view is not exclusive to LeSeur, but considering that her book was published just in 1995, one is tempted to question the reasons and justification for such a classification. One can see how and why LeSeur and others would be tempted to classify *The Suffrage of Elvira* as such but to find peace with such a taxonomic positioning one must be willing to allow for a very liberal, even loose interpretation of what makes a novel a *Bildungsroman.* A wide array of factors regarding characterization in coordination with others undermines any clear-cut categorization of *The Suffrage of Elvira* as a *Bildungsroman.*

There is no gainsaying the fact that since its coinage in 1820 by Karl Morgenstern the *Bildungsroman* has undergone myriad interpretations and convolutions as it has been appropriated and adapted by variant configurations through time and space. And it stands to logic that the claims to the concept of the genre should engender some alteration considering that the circumstances surrounding the *Bildung* of each protagonist must be a reflection of the social, cultural, racial, and political variables of his background. However, most works of fiction that pass as *Bildungsromane* tend to have a number of features that set them apart from mere biographical novels or novels of maturation. According to Morgenstern, "it portrays the *Bildung* of a hero in its beginnings and growth to a certain state of completeness and secondly because it is by virtue of this portrayal that it furthers the reader's *Bildung* to a much greater extent than any other kind of novel."[1] Based on this definition, one quickly notices the sheer gravity placed on the moulding of the protagonist in the novel, as being the sole purpose, and not just an incidental development. Wilhelm Dilthey who believes that the *Bildungsroman* must fulfill certain conditions underscores this point:

> A regulated development within the life of the individual is observed, each of its stages has its own intrinsic value and is at the same time the basis for a higher stage. The dissonances and conflicts of life appear as the necessary growth points through which the individual must pass on his way to maturity and harmony.[2]

It seems obvious that with such emphasis placed on the *Bildung* or the "becoming" of the protagonist, there must be a sense of purpose that transcends the young person's needs for personal growth. As far as Morgenstern is concerned, the protagonist, by virtue of his submission to the molding of the world was supposed to be the model for the German youth who were supposed to tame their individual proclivities and idiosyncrasies by emulating the *Bildungsroman* hero. Of course, we are no longer in nineteenth-century Germany any longer and the expectations that were placed on the young German youth have not been imposed on the non-German world. Writers from regions and cultures far removed from the home of the *Bildungsroman* have appropriated the genre and adapted it to meet the social, political, and cultural imperatives of their configurations with the inevitable consequence of altering the genre both in its form and function. Spatial and temporal variables impose themselves on the creative endeavors of writers, thereby necessitating, in fact, forcing the re-vision of certain established principles or modes of explicating and understanding social phenomena. Hence, although Goethe's *Wilhelm Meister's Apprenticeship* might have, at one time, been upheld as the best fulfillment of the genre, writers today are no longer bound by the same standards or requirements as were Goethe's contemporaries. That is why Todd Kontje's view that "instead of lamenting the non-coincidence of particular novels with an outmoded definition of the genre, we can revitalize our critical awareness of the texts by expanding the boundaries of our discussion [of the *Bildungsroman*]"[3] has a broad appeal especially within postcolonial circles, where the genre has been utilized as a means of articulating the views and aspirations of previously silenced peoples. Writers in third world nations in Africa, Asia, the Caribbean and even oppressed minorities in so-called developed nations have found the *Bildungsroman* to be a viable tool for self-actualization and expression. And why not? Third world writers could not afford to march to the drumbeat of Europe; otherwise they would be endorsing their subaltern position under the imperial hegemony.

All of these factors notwithstanding, can V.S. Naipaul's *The Suffrage of Elvira* stand as a *Bildungsroman* even though he, like most writers of the third world, was not bound by the expectations of the *Goethezeit* conceptualization of the genre? The number of traits that characterize Foreman's growth and maturation in the novel can tempt one into classifying *The Suffrage of Elvira* as a *Bildungsroman* but there are pertinent reasons, even while allowing for the liberal interpretation of what the genre entails, to argue against that taxonomic positioning, and this view does not, in anyway detract from the great merits of the novel. Foreman Baksh does undergo a great deal of maturation in the novel and by its end, he has developed to the point of becoming a household name in Elvira political circles capable of influencing public opinion. However, taking into account the deliberate and conscious nature of the cultivation of the *Bildungsroman* protagonist, it is easy to see lapses in that of Foreman Baksh that might deny him a position among *Bildungsroman* protagonists, if a line is to be drawn in the sand somewhere.

Set in the municipal establishment of Elvira, in which demographic boundaries are blurred along religious, ethnic, and political interest groups, the activities that unfold in this county are indicative of the wave that is sweeping through Trinidad and Tobago as a whole and it is in this mutating atmosphere that we find Foreman, better known as Foam. He is the eldest of seven children of the most influential Muslim in Elvira, Baksh, and this relationship provides him access to circles that are beyond the reach of his peers. The circle of influence in Elvira includes Baksh, Chittaranjan, Dhaniram the pundit, as well as the political candidates, Mr. Surujpat Harbans and Preacher, and to a lesser degree, Teacher Francis. Apart from their relative wealthy status, these people are also set apart by their ages; most of them are in their middle ages, except for Harbans, the candidate, who is older. Foam and Lockhoor form the up-and-coming generation who are liable to learn the lessons of life from the elders. Knowing the older generation in terms of their moral standing in the community, one must wonder what Foreman would learn from them and what he would become as a consequence.

The first description of Foam portrays him, at least in Harbans' eyes as a young man with a "tall and wiry body" who is "a little arrogant" and whose "booming voice made him almost as frightening as his father" (17). As a high school drop-out, he has been assisting in his father's tailoring workshop but he has not been allowed to do more than tack coats. Typically, the *Bildungsroman* protagonist is portrayed as standing out in some trait, either in academic performance or among his peers and is generally younger than Foam at the beginning of his quest for selfhood. Because most of them tend to be dissatisfied with their stations in life and are powerless to effect meaningful change, they leave in anger as acts of rebellion against the status quo. This is often precipitated by disagreements or fights with their fathers more so than by their inability to transform their youthful idealism into some form of practical reality. As far as *The Suffrage of Elvira* is concerned, Foam does not seem to nurse any strong resentment concerning his place in the family apart from a transient venting of frustration over his limited role in his father's workshop and over having to live at home under his controlling mother. In spite of these, Foam is thrust into the political arena by his crafty father as a campaign manager for Mr. Harbans and there begins his political 'education.' Without a mentor or a formal teacher to guide him, Foam forges ahead, learning by trial and error, and from observing and listening to the ever-changing positions of the elders, including that of his father.

At home, Foreman assumes his responsibility as the eldest child quite well by protecting the interests of his younger siblings. When Mrs. Baksh in her rage beats up Herbert for bringing home the stray dog named Tiger, Foam steps in.

> Then Foam called in his stern booming voice, 'All right, Ma.'
> Mrs. Baksh stopped and looked at him.
> Baksh looked at him.
> Mechanically Mrs. Baksh passed the belt back to Baksh.
> Herbert sat on the steps, his eyes and nose streaming. His sobs, half snuffle and half snort, came at regular intervals.
> Tiger dozed on, his ears twitching.
> Mrs. Baksh sat down on the chair, exhausted, and began to cry. 'My own son, my biggest son, talking to me so!' (72)

This intervention is a statement of Foam's maturation and awareness of the power that is attendant with his position as firstborn, and his willingness to confront his mother is indicative of his sense of selfhood as an adult, no longer as a child. Mrs. Baksh's shock at hearing her son speak to her with such a tone breaks her down but that is a step she must deal with as a parent. The threat of the loss of parental authority over her first son is painful for her, however later on in the novel, when Baksh jumps ship on Harbans in favour of Preacher, Foam remains faithful to Harbans: "'All right, you support Preacher,' Foam said, and Mrs. Baksh noted that for the first time Foam was talking to his father man-to-man" (139). Although the reader is not provided with any editorial comment here, it is highly plausible that Mrs. Baksh's approves of this development of her son. That Foam is no longer a boy to be ordered around but can now take part in political matters among men without compromising his own views must be pleasing to Mrs. Baksh and to the reader as well.

Even among his siblings, one notices the role Foam plays in protecting Herbert from punishment and in his assistance to Herbert in nursing Tiger the dog to good health. It is, therefore, safe to assert that despite his failure as a student by which he became a negative model for his younger siblings, Foam has attained a sense of selfhood as a young man, capable of taking decisions that may contravene those of his parents. These domestic milestones are crucial for they signal Foam's readiness for the challenges of politics in which people are willing to wallow in mud as far as their selfish aspirations are fulfilled. He might not have a great model at home but he has undergone psychological growth and can hold his own in the public arena.

Knowing Foam's father, it is easy to deduce that Foam has not received any strong moral lessons at home and so he is most likely to surrender to the winds of time. And that is why he does not object to the chicanery of which his father is a strong part. Mr. Baksh's political ambition is limited to and controlled by his greed; he looks for personal profit, not for the good of the Muslim community, and all but coerces Harbans into taking Foam as his campaign manager for a salary.

Mr. Surujpat Harbans exhibits very weak characteristics either as a person or as a candidate. His near rustic appearance is further undermined by the vapidity of his personality. Easily cowered into decisions and stances on issues by varying interest groups, he lacks the fortitude of mind and spirit that would inspire anyone around to revere him, despite his elderly status and so it is evident that he cannot be a model for Foam. Harbans' first sight of Foam frightens him and there is no time in the novel when Mr Harbans exhibits any wisdom or character to attract Foam's or anyone else's respect. His superstitious mind causes him to be dogged by fears of what treachery the future holds for him. The pundit Dhaniram is really no better than Baksh because his own political interest is wrapped around personal gain. Dependent on the *Doolahin*, his runaway son's wife for domestic chores that include caring for his paralyzed wife, Dhaniram is more excited by the new lexicon that has entered the repertoire of Elvira thanks to the onset of democracy than he is in any position on matters of importance to the people looking up to him. The same is true of Chittaranjan, who sees Mr. Harban's candidacy as an opportunity for him to orchestrate his daughter's marriage to Mr. Harban's son, who is a medical student in England. With the county of Elvira in the hands of men such as these, it is highly unlikely that Foam would find any of them worthy of emulating. With the overlay of superstition over people's sense of safety and security, a dimension of the absurd is brought to bear on the development of Foam's selfhood, thereby complicating matters as the lines between the rational and irrational are further blurred. His *Bildung*, if it must be accomplished, would be in spite of mentorship, not thanks to it for there are no morally upright figures in Elvira and the political game is one in which the end justifies the means and not vice-versa.

At the first convergence of the movers and shakers of the burgeoning political campaign for Mr. Harbans, Foam finds himself in the house of the most influential Hindu in Elvira, Chittaranjan, whose big house is the talk of Elvira. It is a meeting to map out strategies on how to counter the effectiveness of the Hindu sellout, Lorkhoor, who has mounted a fairly effective campaign for Preacher. Although the reader by this juncture in the novel has just about given up hope of seeing the characters rise up to some moral high ground, the sight of the framed picture of the most venerable Mahatma Gandhi raises expectations of some degree of conscientiousness.

> [...] Harbans saw a large framed picture of the Round Table Conference with King George V and Mahatma Gandhi sitting together, the King formally dressed and smiling, the Mahatma in a loincloth, also smiling. The picture made Harbans easier. He himself had a picture like that in his drawing-room in Port of Spain (33).

Knowing Mahatma Gandhi, a man of legendary integrity,

courage, and intelligence, the sight of his framed picture in one of the most triumphant moments of his fight for Indian independence would engender expectations that Mr. Harbans would be inspired by the same traits for which Gandhi was revered. The easy feeling that Harbans experiences generates hopes that he rises up to the occasion and express some ideological position relative to the needs of his prospective constituency, but unfortunately the hope is woefully dashed. Gandhi's picture hanging on the wall, overlooking the deliberations provides nothing but a counter point, a stark contrast to Harbans. Harbans may have the same picture in his home in Port of Spain and he may be comforted by his physical closeness to the same in Chittaranjan's drawing room, but he is at best an ideological agnostic, the best example of what Gandhi was not. Whether he wins the election or not, it seems apparent even this early in the campaign that the fortunes of the Indians, Blacks, Muslims, and Spaniards would not, in any way change for the better. In the amoral atmosphere of Trinidad and Tobago, the quest for political office is devoid of any political commitment and the 'players' are no more than tricksters, who are willing to clinch deals with any entity, regardless of its moral standing. No judgment is passed concerning any character or action; the only concern is the correlation of the individual and the action to the outcome of the votes. That is the world in which Foam's maturity takes place, and he has learned his tricks well.

In his first effort to leave a mark on the political landscape of Elvira, the campaign manager Foam plunges enthusiastically into the fray, not so much for the sake of Harbans, who is paying him a salary for this role, as for his desire to avenge the loss of his position to Lorkhoor as campaign manager for movie theatres. Foam is fuelled essentially by the need to assuage the dent on his ego by Lorkhoor, and he is no better than the older generation who are now trying to assume the helm of government in the new democracy. Lorkhoor, the better-educated and better-spoken rival to Foam's ambition is no more redeeming in his character than Foam. Because the older generation failed to be inspired by Gandhi into having a sense of commitment to the needs of their constituents, they are incapable of transmitting any meaningful example to Foam and his generation. This sad situation is further aggravated by the fact that all of them, the older and the younger generations are trying their hands at a game that is completely new to them. There are no models in Trinidad and Tobago for them to follow and Foam is as good or bad as they are. Perhaps, the best summation of the situation is by Foam himself, as he tries to cheer up the bashful Harbans on their way to court Chittaranjan's support. "'Way I see it is this. In Trinidad this democracy is a brand new thing. We is still creeping. We is a creeping nation [...]. I respect people like you, you know, Mr. Harbans, doing this thing for the first time'" (27). In other words, the young Foam and the older Harbans are like old and young circus monkeys, except that both of them are learning new tricks together.

Protagonists of the *Bildungsroman* are often confronted and challenged by situations in which their moral fibre is put to the test within a larger framework in which people are tested in similar ways on a regular basis. The choices made by the protagonists under those circumstances often become important in determining their progress towards selfhood or the lack thereof. If Foam were a *Bildungsroman* protagonist, his self-awareness and his moral sensitivity would have engendered a rebellion against the mess into which the community is plunged. But without any moral consideration over anybody or any action, Foam has no moral yardstick by which to measure his own acts or those of the elders of his community and no moral compass by which to orientate his future. Whether or not the non-judgmental stance of the novel is a reflection on the poor craftsmanship of V.S. Naipaul or not is not the focus of this paper, however, if Naipaul, in including Foreman Baksh in the novel intended to have a *Bildungsprozess* as a backdrop to the suffrage of the county of Elvira, then his outcome was less than spectacular. The satirical nature of the novel itself seems to undermine any intent for the character of Foam, in fact, all the characters, to be taken too seriously. Although Naipaul has been subjected to acrimonious vilification for the amoral portrayal of characters in *The Suffrage of Elvira*, one is inclined to lean more to the more sympathetic but no less accurate stance taken by Richard Kelly:

> It might be more reasonable to argue, at least from the young Naipaul's point of view, that Trinidad afforded precious little life for its inhabitants [...]. Indeed, [Naipaul] fails to invest any of his early characters with a fundamental goodness and depth of feeling [...]. Naipaul's characters are morally neutral—incapable of great evil or great good because they are living on a plain where cleverness, agility, appearance, stupidity, wit, and conniving seem sufficient to keep them going.[4]

Harping on the opportunity missed by the leaders to emulate Mahatma Gandhi and thereby elevate the Indian peoples of the West Indies to better conditions, Cudjoe cautions that the new experience of

> the people of Elvira can be a progressive social phenomenon only if it is used in a constructive manner rather than to manipulate prejudices, disguise false sentiments, or perpetuate obsolete superstitious practices. It can be accomplished only if the people truly accept the principles manifested in the life and practices of Mahatma Gandhi in his struggle to attain *Swaraj* in their ancestral home.[5]

In spite of this disappointing denouement to the novel, as far as Foam's supposed *Bildungsprozess* is concerned, it still seems plausible to have some hope that the world that Foam and his generation are inheriting would be better than that of the older generation, if for nothing else than the fact that the overwhelming belief in superstition would cease to be a factor in their own cosmology. Having seen the emptiness of that arcane worldview right at home with the presence of Tiger and the commotion that was generated by his father, it is reassuring to know that Foam, his younger brother Herbert, and the rest of the youthful populace would relegate the fear of "obeah"[6] to realm of quaint mythology. However, if Foam pursues his political ambition, one fears that although he would be more charismatic and savvy than Harbans, he would be no better than him in terms of moral values.

Notes

1. Quoted in Martin Swales, *The German Bildungsroman from Wieland to Hesse* (Princeton: Princeton UP, 1978) 12.
2. Swales 3.
3. Todd Kontje, "The Bildungsroman as Metafiction," *Michigan Germanic Studies* 8 (1987): 140-55.
4. Richard Kelly, *V.S. Naipaul* (New York: Continuum, 1989) 52.
5. Selwyn R. Cudjoe, *V.S. Naipaul: A Materialist Reading* (Amherst: U of Massachusetts P, 1988) 49-50.
6. An occult practice common in the West Indies by which people are believed to be hurt.

Work Cited

Cudjoe, Selwyn R. *V.S. Naipaul: A Materialist Reading*. Amherst: U of Massachusetts P, 1988.

Kelly, Richard. *V.S. Naipaul*. New York: Continuum, 1989.

Kontje, Todd Curtis. "The Bildungsroman as Metafiction." *Michigan Germanic Studies* 8 (1987): 140-55.

Leseur, Geta J. *Ten Is the Age of Darkness: the Black Bildungsroman*. Columbia: U of Missouri P, 1995.

Naipaul, V.S. *The Suffrage of Elvira*. London: Andre Deutch, 1958.

Swales, Martin. *The German Bildungsroman from Wieland to Hesse*. Princeton, N.J.: Princeton UP, 1978.

CONTRIBUTORS

Thieme, John : English/HSS, South Bank University, London SE1 0AA UK.

Khanna, Stuti : K-L/74, Kavi Nagar, Ghaziabad 201 002 Uttar Pradesh, India.

Ciompi, Fausto : Dipartimento di Anglistica, Università di Pisa, Via S. Maria 67 56126 Pisa, Italy.

D'Souza, Florence : English Department, University of Lille 3, BP 149, 59653 VILLENEUVE D'ASCQ Cédex, France.

Leusmann, Harald : Department of English, Ball State University, Muncie, IN 47306 USA.

Roldán-Santiago, Serafín : Urb La Plata, Calle Rubi L-12, Cayey, Puerto Rico 00736.

Baneth-Nouailhetas, Emilienne : University of Paris III – Sorbonne Nouvelle, CNRS – Laboratoire Intermedia, Institut du Monde anglophone, 5 rue de l'Ecole de Médecine, Paris.

Buma, Pascal P. : Department of English, The University of Akron, Akron, OH 44325-1906 USA.